Into the Far Country

Into the Far Country

*A Theology of Mission
for an Age of Violence*

Tom Stuckey

EPWORTH

British Library Cataloguing in Publication data

A catalogue record for this book is available from the British Library

Bible quotations are taken from the *New International Version*, copyright © 1973, 1978, 1984 by the International Bible Society, published by Hodder and Stoughton; and the *Revised Standard Version* © 1971 and 1952 by the National Council of the Churches of Christ in the USA

978 0 7162 0574 6

First published in 2003
by Epworth Press
4 John Wesley Road
Werrington
Peterborough PE4 6ZP

Second impression 2007

Printed and bound in Great Britain by
William Clowes Ltd, Beccles, Suffolk

Contents

Contents

Foreword

The more I think about it, the more I am coming to realize that one of the great graces that has been given to the Catholic diocese of Portsmouth has been its 'twinning' with the diocese of Bamenda in Cameroon. The relationship was set up by one of my predecessors, not simply so that we could help a developing diocese in a developing country, but – and perhaps principally – so that we could develop an understanding of the Church which transcended national boundaries and cultures.

It has been my privilege to visit Bamenda four times during my time as Bishop and each time I have done so, I have returned home much more acutely aware of the essential nature and task of the Church being rooted in 'communion' and 'mission'. That 'communion' is far from being rooted in the uniformity that might be pleasing to the Vatican and the sense of 'mission' goes much deeper and wider than simply making people Catholic Christians.

Pope Paul VI, in his seminal encyclical *Evangelii Nuntiandi*, describes evangelization as 'bringing the Good News into all strata of humanity, and through its influence transforming humanity from within and making it new'.[1] 'That is a vision which demands that the Church – and Christians – recognize that we are servants of the Word and that the Word has a dynamism and power which belongs to God and which is subject to the Spirit, the wind which blows where it pleases; you can hear its sound but you cannot tell where it comes from or where it is going. So it is with everyone who is born of the Spirit.'[2]

Into the Far Country has much of the Spirit in it. I have found it refreshing and life giving. Like its author, who is a valued and precious colleague in our community of churches in Hampshire, it challenges and stimulates. In some ways, Tom Stuckey is sharing with us an extended meditation on the parable of the 'prodigal son' or 'lost son' and the words that always strike home for me in that Lucan story are those spoken by the son himself when he says, 'I must leave this place and go to my Father.'[3] With his insights and out of his experience, Tom is challenging all of us to conversion in the truest sense, to leave the place where we are, so that we can return to the Word and then allow its imperative to transform our communities and congregations.

To return again, if I may, to Pope Paul VI. He writes, 'Modern man listens more willingly to witnesses than to teachers, and if he does listen to teachers, it is because they are witnesses.'[4] Tom Stuckey is a teacher but these pages leave us in no doubt at all that he is also a witness.

Two books have particularly stimulated my reflections during this year. The first has been *The Dignity of Difference*, by Jonathan Sacks, which Tom quotes in Chapter 4, and the second is *Into the Far Country*, which I hope you will enjoy and be as enlightened by as I have been.

Bishop Crispian Hollis
Bishop of Portsmouth

Prologue

During my teens I developed a passionate interest in theology. From the moment of hearing the call to preach I became aware of the importance of biblical revelation and fascinated by the challenge of making the Word accessible to those on the edges of the Church. Since entering the Methodist ministry in 1964 I have worked at different frontiers of mission, serving in a mining community, a new town, a difficult housing estate, a city centre church and as a part-time university chaplain. In 1982 I was appointed Tutor in Applied Theology within the Northern Federation for Training in Ministry, Manchester, taught theology of mission and served as a minister of a multi-racial congregation in the inner city.

As a lecturer, I was able to address in a more systematic way some of the difficulties I had encountered over the 20 years of ministering in a Church which, when not preoccupied with itself, functioned with an inadequate theology of mission. In 1987 I visited India and gave the Abraham Malpan Lectures in the Mar Thoma Church.[1] This, together with a stay in Sri Lanka and a short teaching spell in Malaysia, raised fresh questions.

Still uneasy with our current practices of ministerial formation, I left my teaching post and became Methodist superintendent of a large circuit where I was able to put into practice some of the things I had learnt about theological reflection and mission. Over the years I have written articles and been on many working parties.[2] In 1998 I was appointed to my present post as Chair of the Southampton Methodist

District. A sabbatical and visit to South Africa in the spring of 2001 gave me the opportunity to refine my thinking in this book.

Thanks are due to many people: my former colleagues and students within the Northern Federation for Training in Ministry, Manchester; those I met in India, Sri Lanka, Malaysia and South Africa; my friends in the Southern Theological Education and Training Scheme at Salisbury; the countless people in the Methodist circuits from whom over the years I have learnt so much. I am particularly grateful to Revd Ross Olivier from the Methodist Church of Southern Africa. His perceptive suggestions have led me to reorder and rewrite sections of what follows. I similarly wish to thank Revd Gerald Burt and the Epworth Press for their astute comments on the draft manuscript, the editorial staff of SCM Press and Revd Eric Renouf for his careful perusal of the text. I am also indebted to the Hampshire Church Leaders: their helpful criticisms give some balance to the final chapters.

I am delighted that my friend the Rt Revd Crispian Hollis, Roman Catholic Bishop of the Diocese of Portsmouth, agreed to write the Foreword. Over the years I have come to appreciate the important influence of Catholic spirituality upon the Wesleys.[3] The contribution of some contemporary Roman Catholics to my own theological understanding of mission is not inconsiderable as this book will demonstrate.

I would have given up writing on several occasions had it not been for the enthusiasm and support of Professor Mary Grey who deserves special mention. My biggest thank you must of course be to my wife Christine whose love and enduring patience remain a constant source of encouragement.

Tom Stuckey

Into the far country

I

What is mission?
Into the far country

All authority in heaven and on earth has been given to me. Go therefore and make disciples of all nations, baptizing them in the name of the Father and of the Son and of the Holy Spirit, teaching them to observe all that I have commanded you; and lo, I am with you always to the close of the age. (Matt. 28.18–20)

What is mission? When this question was asked in a seminar on mission there was a stream of suggestions.

Mission is planting a new congregation, building a hospital, starting a play-group, extending a church building, working with the homeless, planning an evangelistic crusade, fighting for justice, preaching the word, setting up an Alpha Group, establishing partnerships, holding an open-air meeting for worship, liberating the oppressed, uniting churches, sharing the good news of Jesus Christ, making wise use of resources, deepening the spiritual life, making disciples, financing a project to supply water in an African village, winning the world for Christ, meeting with Muslims for dialogue, setting up a Christian school.

The list is endless. 'Mission' is such a slippery word.

Professor Thomas Thangaraj, whom I first met in South India, points out that the word 'mission' is no longer the private property of Christian discourse.[1] It has become a public word used by national governments and popularized by the fictional character of James Bond 007. The current practice, found in secular corporations and institutions, of formulating 'mission statements' has now prompted many maintenance-bound churches to do the same.

The great commission and the great compassion

The word 'mission' comes from the Latin *mittere* meaning 'to send' and therefore describes almost any situation in which there is either some actual or desired movement from one condition to another. Matthew 10 describes how Jesus sent out the 12 disciples to preach, heal the sick, raise the dead, cleanse those with leprosy and drive out demons. In Luke's version, 70 (Lk. 10.1) are sent out in twos with a similar mandate. They travel light and move fast in a hit-and-run exercise, like door-to-door salesmen. This is but a trial run for the main campaign, for when empowered by the Holy Spirit the disciples become apostles. These apostles, from the Greek word *apostolos* meaning a 'sent person', are now instructed to go into the 'far country' as witnesses of Christ (Acts 1.8). Mission describes movement. It promotes change.

The Roman Catholic Church has always had a missionary dimension. The Protestant Reformers, however, believed that the missionary mandate only applied to the apostolic period. The strong emphasis on the Holy Spirit within Lutheran Pietism put mission back on the agenda. Under the leadership of Count Ludwig von Zinzendorf (1700–60) the missionary passion of Moravian Christians was revived and expressed in practical ways as they carried the gospel into the Americas and from Greenland to the 'far country' of South Africa.[2] William Carey is regarded by many Protestants as 'the father of modern missions'.[3] He wrote a book with the catchy title *An Enquiry into the Obligations of Christians to use Means for the Conversion of the Heathen*. The title is an indication of the difficulty he faced. Since his fellow Calvinists believed conversion to be God's own work, there was nothing much human beings could do about it. Carey disagreed. His methodical study of the Scriptures and careful examination of Church history led him back to Matthew 28.18–20 which heads this chapter.

This 'great commission', he argued, is a divine mandate and therefore must be obeyed. In a powerful sermon in Nottingham on 31 May 1792, he castigated the congregation for their lack of obedience to the divine command and is reputed to have uttered the famous words, 'Attempt great things for God; expect great things from God.' There was little response and so he himself set off for the 'far country' of India.

In 1735, a disillusioned John Wesley, hoping that 'Primitive Christianity' could be recovered, and that he would find full salvation for himself and others in some idealized Garden of Eden, set off for the 'far country' of Georgia in America. It was a life-changing trip because he fell under the spell of the Moravians.[4] His search for a living faith 'which none can have without knowing that he hath it' was to lead him on 24 May 1738 to a little society in Aldersgate Street where 'his heart was strangely warmed'.[5] However, the decisive moment for Wesley's engagement in mission came a year later when, following an invitation from George Whitefield, he began 'field preaching'. On 2 April 1739 he 'submitted to be more vile' and went into another 'far country', stepping out into the open air and preaching to about three thousand colliers in Kingswood, Bristol.[6]

Matthew 28.18–20 has become the mission 'magna carta' of evangelicals. Nevertheless this text is only one of many passages of Scripture applicable to the missionary task. Wesley preached his first open air sermon on Luke 4.18–19, a text which has since prompted understandings of mission as liberation and social concern. Both William Carey and John Wesley had a world vision. Charles Wesley set the Methodist mission to music:

> O that the world might taste and see
> The riches of his grace!
> The arms of love that compass me
> Would all mankind embrace.[7]

John Wesley's heroic endeavours were inspired by the vision of the Spirit of God burning first like a flame in the hearts of converted individuals, then firing communities and blazing like a mighty forest fire until scriptural holiness covered the whole earth. The Spirit was given by a compassionate Father who wished to include all in his loving embrace. The theological incentive for Methodism's overseas mission sprang from the belief that the conversion of the world was part of the purpose of God because the Son would glorify the Father only when the lost sheep were brought home. These lost sheep were the peoples of all nations who were at present deprived of their natural birthright.[8]

In Luke 15 we have three parables about mission. The first two, the parables of the 'lost sheep' and the 'lost coin', focus on the God who goes in search of the lost. The third, the parable of the 'lost son' focuses on 'the waiting father'.[9] The phrase is an unfortunate one for it implies passivity. A similar passivity is present in Raymond Fung's comment that the contemporary Church should, like the father in the story, wait until an economically bankrupt and spiritually exhausted modern culture prompts a return of people to the fold.[10] While the father did not physically go into the 'far country' his active grace never abandoned his son but eventually lured him back to life. The father's 'embrace' seeks to draw in, not only the younger but also the elder son who although at home had become lost in his own 'far country'. The compassionate grace of this loving father, in Wesley's words, 'embraces all mankind'. A theology of mission has to be inclusive.

First interlude: there and back again

During my time in Manchester when preparing courses on 'mission', I became increasingly interested in the creative and distinctive contribution of Third World theologians such as Tissa Balasuriya, Aloysius Pieris, Zacharias Mar Theophilius, Bede Griffiths, Choan-Seng Song, Kosuke Koyama, Ahn Byung-Mu, John Mbiti and Orlando Costas. I found myself asking, 'Should I not spend some period in a far country?' My mind had been conditioned to think in Western categories, and I suspected that I was probably not hearing what the Eastern theologians were saying. Would I discover wisdom if I followed in the steps of William Carey and travelled to India? Could I talk with Bede Griffiths who had journeyed there more recently and whose writings puzzled me?[11] Having recently read Thomas Merton's *Asian Journal*[12] and been moved by his account of the visit to Polonnaruwa in Sri Lanka, I resolved that my journey would not only be an exploration of mission but also be a spiritual journey. I wanted to gaze as Merton did, on the great stone carvings of the Buddha. Maybe in the silence of their extraordinary faces I too would catch a glimpse of the wisdom and serenity that had touched him so deeply. These were the glimmerings of an idea which launched my sabbatical visit to India and Sri Lanka in June 1987.

The 'far country' affected me deeply for I found in the friendliness, deportment and dignity of the people a simple joy and grace which we in this country seem to lack. On my return, Christianity in Britain appeared drab when compared with the visual vivaciousness of the East. I now had further questions. More importantly, I came back with a changed perspective because of experiences I had not sought. In my journal, I wrote:

> To spend six hours each day for nearly a week in silent meditation with Buddhists high in the central hills of Sri Lanka rather exposes the deficiencies of one's prayer life. To live with the poor in a hot, parched jungle village and do theological reflection with Father Michael Rodrigo is to gain new vision. To give the Abraham Malpan memorial lectures in Kottayam, South India, before some of the most prominent academics in Kerala, and then to be taken to task by bishops of the Mar Thoma Church is a sobering experience. To preach to 2000 people at an ordination service of the Church of South India is good for the ego, but to listen

to the victims of the ethnic conflict in Sri Lanka is to become aware of a new and terrible meaning to sin and suffering.

I suggested that the majority of Christians in Britain continue to assume that Christianity has come to replace other faiths. Our question has therefore been, how can we win the world for Christ? After hundreds of years of evangelistic effort we are still no nearer that goal. Only about a third of the total population of the world is Christian.[13] Should we not instead be asking, what is the role of Christianity in a world of other faiths and ideologies?

What sort of God?

How we actually practice mission says a lot about the sort of God we believe in. To give a quick and rather extreme example: in the early 1700s most Western Christians believed that God had made the person they labelled 'negro' an inferior creature, a descendant of the accursed Ham.[14] With breathtaking smugness Gilbert Burnet, Bishop of Salisbury, argued that because slaves in the Caribbean had contributed so much to Britain it was only right and proper that they should receive the benefits of Christianity.[15] In 1712 the Society for the Propagation of the Christian Gospel was bequeathed a sugar plantation in Barbados. Each of the slaves was branded on the chest with the word 'Society' to denote their new owner. It is hardly surprising, given such treatment, that the number of conversions to Christianity was small. This savage demonstration of missionary practice not only originates from a corrosive mixture of culture and gospel but suggests that the God who condones such torment must be cruel, cold and inhuman. Our missionary practice must accurately reflect our understanding of the God of mission.

For many, who sit in the pews on Sunday, 'mission' describes a 'sending' activity of the Church. At the World Missionary Conference of 1952 held in Willingen, West Germany, this popular notion was turned on its head through the growing realization that mission was not 'ours' but 'God's'.[16] That conference revived a very ancient phrase, *missio Dei* – the 'mission of God'. Karl Barth had argued that *missio Dei* was a more accurate way of speaking of the Church's mission.[17] The term had also been used hundreds of years earlier in discussions about the Trinity. Following Willingen, missiology has absorbed the understanding of 'mission' as 'the mission of the God who is Father, Son and Holy Spirit'.[18] Our thinking about mission cannot therefore be divorced from our thinking about the Trinity; indeed the latter takes precedence over the former.

This book addresses the 'who' and the 'what' of mission. Unlike many books on this subject which focus mainly on the second question, I seek to integrate explicitly 'what we do' in mission with our understanding of 'the God' of mission. This is where covenant comes in. Covenant is a relational concept reflecting the dynamic life of the Trinity, so the idea of 'covenant partners' permeates the pages of this book. Three sets of double chapters explore the mission of the triune God. Chapters 2 and 3 focus on the universal Father and the covenant with Noah, Chapters 4 and 5 on the particularity of the Son and the covenant with Abraham, whilst Chapters 6 and 7 centre on the Holy Spirit and the new covenant of brokenness and blessing established in Jesus Christ.

Because God is a Trinitarian God of grace, this book sets the 'great commission' of Matthew 28.18–20 in the context of the 'great compassion' of Luke 15. So Chapters 3, 5 and 7 provide three opportunities within this Trinitarian framework, for interpreting the 'great commission'. In the last two chapters, I shall attempt a definitive answer to my opening question, what is mission?

When I began this book some years ago, the twin towers of the World Trade Center in New York stood witnessing to a confident global economy. Since 9/11 storm clouds have rolled over the horizon. An early Bible story describes how God looked at the earth and was overcome with grief (Gen. 6.6). The words 'the earth was corrupt in God's sight and full of violence' (6.11) now resonate with contemporary relevance. The optimism which marked the celebration of the new millennium is no more. We appear to have entered an age of violence. As Gil Bailie prophetically announces in his book *Violence Unveiled*, 'humanity stands at the crossroads'.[19] Our understanding of the task of mission therefore needs to undergo some reconstruction if we are to witness in a world of violence. Thankfully the Genesis text, quoted above, is but a pessimistic prelude to a rainbow covenant story of hope.

What sort of book?

People stumble over the word 'theology'. 'Theology' is derived from the Greek words *logos*, meaning 'reasoning' and *theos* the word for 'God'. 'Theology is the methodical interpretation of the contents of the Christian faith,' writes Paul Tillich.[20] Our construction of a theology of mission based on the Trinity begins with the Bible, but not the Bible alone. Methodist theologians speak of the 'Wesleyan quadrilateral'.[21] Scripture has always been read through particular lenses: Wesley named these as 'tradition', 'reason' and 'experience'. There was no fixed balance between them. 'While scripture remained basic, the influence of these lenses on his [Wesley's] exposition of specific doctrines varied over time.'[22] This creates a fluidity enabling theology to be shaped by the Holy Spirit and by the culture of the age. We shall see in the following chapters that the pressure from culture is not insignificant. Indeed it has often had a detrimental effect on our Western theological perspectives as illustrated in the Barbados story. While the requirement of 'reason' is self-evident, something needs to be said about 'tradition and experience'.

We can no longer limit these to 'Christian tradition' and 'Christian experience'. In our conversations about mission we now meet and talk with Jews, Muslims, Buddhists and others. I am suggesting that the concept of 'experience' be enlarged to include the experience of those 'outside the Christian tradition'. Whilst the Bible is the starting point for us, it is not so for them. Indeed the Bible is also a forgotten book for most people in the once-Christian West. Thomas Thangaraj[23] would argue that starting with the Bible and the Trinitarian *missio Dei* excludes most people from meaningful theological dialogue. He is probably right, but he is addressing a different audience from that which I am addressing. I am writing for those Christian ministers, priests and lay persons in Britain, South Africa and North America who are searching for a new theological framework out of which to engage in meaningful mission for the twenty-first century. My purpose is to encourage the Church to move into the 'far country' where such conversations proposed by Thomas Thangaraj can take place. My aim is to show that if we are to engage in mission, the 'centre' of the Church must be the 'edge'.

Secondly, I refer to 'experience' in the more traditional Wesleyan sense of the personal and inward witness of the Spirit.[24] This theology of mission will, in Chapters 2, 4 and 6, be punctuated by 'interludes' of autobiographical material. You may wish to pass quickly over these extracts from my journal. I include them because for me, mission, spiritual journey and theological exploration are inseparable. My personal journey to the 'far country' has reshaped my understanding of the God of mission. I invite you to travel with me. I also include these personal references both to lighten the theological content and to encourage the reader to make connections between theology, practical ministry and personal experience.[25] Whether these 'interludes' help or hinder is for you to judge. To aid theological reflection in a church-group setting I have, in the Appendix, set out some suggestions and questions. I hope these will not only sharpen up discussion but also motivate you into mission.

While Karl Barth's influence upon me is substantial, I have in recent years increasingly come to value the theological approach of John Wesley.[26] His understanding of mission has such a contemporary ring that I have tried, in writing these pages, to draw on his spirit. Let this book stand as my own contribution to the celebration of the tercentenary of his birth.

Every author has to decide what to do about sexist language. My response to this, apart from quotations, has simply been to try to eliminate the words 'he' and 'she'. I have not entirely succeeded so I have used these pronouns in a random fashion. When referring to God I have, with some unease, mainly used the traditional masculine pronoun throughout. I believe that God embraces both male and female genders within him/herself and yet at the same time transcends gender.

Lessons from the far country

2

The rainbow covenant

When I bring the clouds over the earth and the bow is seen in the clouds, I will remember my covenant which is between me and you and every living creature of all flesh; and the waters shall never again become a flood to destroy all flesh. (Gen. 9.14–15)

Mission begins with God. Mission is in God. Mission is about partnership because God is Trinity and Trinity reflects the relational idea of persons in communion. This idea of partnership in God and with God is expressed in the Bible by a theology of 'covenants'. A covenant is a contractual arrangement whereby two or more partners bind themselves to each other for their mutual benefit. Covenants are embracing, open ended and elastic enough to accommodate the shifts and failures of the partners. In contrast, a contract is essentially utilitarian based on a 'reductionist abstraction of persons' and therefore does not take account of the fluidity of human existence.[1] The gospel is founded on gracious covenants not legal contracts.

A covenant of grace

Theology in the early part of the twentieth century was dominated by the figure of Karl Barth. Covenant stands at the centre of his theology. God the creator calls his creatures to participate in his own glory. 'I will be your God and you shall be my people.'[2] According to Barth, God's choice of us is an act of pure grace and its goal is the restoration of the divine image in humankind.[3] To this end God calls us to be his covenant partners in Jesus Christ.[4] Mission, therefore, is not derived from a particular concept of history which threatens us with damnation. Neither does it arise because of human sinfulness or idolatry. Mission is necessary because a loving God wants us to be his partners in service. Barth, at a single stroke, removes every legal argument and human justification for mission. We engage in mission because God in his grace invites us to do so.

God's relationship with us has been likened to that of an author trying to write a novel.[5] The author sits in front of a blank sheet of paper. It is a terrifying moment; something may be started which can never be finished. Will the author be able to manage the material she creates, for the generated text seems to acquire a life of its own? The author, as a creative artist, can only respond to the way the story goes. There will be those agonizing moments when the writer is 'blocked' and left wondering in her disappointment and frustration whether to rip it all up and start again.

By calling us into a partnership with himself, God does not stand above the covenant but in it; yet he is not under it. It is always 'his' covenant.[6] Moreover, in deciding to work with humanity he has chosen some very unpredictable material. Unlike a human contract which can release one partner if the other defaults, God has pledged himself to keep his side of the bargain even if we break ours. The binding nature of this covenant is such that neither God nor humanity can reach their goal without the other. God has therefore to improvise as he goes along (Hos. 1.10–11). If we give up, the story becomes blocked. The author of history can only wait until we return and this waiting is a very painful business:

> How can I give you up, O Ephraim! How can I hand you over, O Israel! How can I make you like Admah! How can I treat you like Zeboim! My heart recoils within me, my compassion grows warm and tender. (Hos. 11.8f.)

The gender image of God becomes specifically female in a New Testament passage describing this God who waits:

How often would I have gathered your children together as a hen gathers her brood under her wings, and you would not. (Matt. 23.37)

When a theology of mission is set within the covenant of grace, the traditional metaphysical concepts of omnipotence, omniscience and omnipresence break down. God can no longer be described in terms of 'substance' or 'absolute subject',[7] or always given a masculine gender. This triune God of grace is an interactive, creative, imaginative, community God who suffers, undergoes change, gets frustrated, experiences pain and exemplifies love. Barth, in the section entitled 'The Way of the Son of God into the Far Country', tells us that the omnipotence of this God is such that he who is strong has chosen to be weak; he who is invincible has chosen to be vulnerable.[8] When a theology of mission is founded on a covenant of grace, humanity becomes caught up in the greatest love story ever told.

Miroslav Volf, in his exposition of the parable of the lost son, illuminates this love story through his use of the word 'embrace' (Lk. 15.11–32).[9] A covenant 'embraces' with a mutuality of loving; a contract is a chain which binds or breaks. In the Bible, if one partner breaks the covenant the other suffers the breach because God's covenant cannot be undone. When the younger son goes off into the 'far country' the father does not cease to have a second son; rather he becomes the father of the 'lost' or 'dead' son, even though the son has tried to 'un-son' himself. When the son remembers his 'son-ship' (v. 17) and comes home, the father's 'embrace' expresses inclusion. The elder son, employing a high moral tone, does not realize that by placing 'rules' above 'relationships' he excludes himself. In this parable the choice is 'embrace' or 'exclude'. Contracts can exclude; a covenant is always open to the inclusion of all. 'Embrace is the inner side of the covenant and the covenant is the outer side of embrace.'[10]

The Old Testament focuses primarily on God's particular

partnership with Israel initiated through his covenant with Abraham and demonstrated supremely in the event of the Exodus. This relationship with Israel takes historical and theological precedence so that the Noachic and Patriarchal sagas appear to have been written to show how Israel came to be God's chosen people. Yet God's life-affirming mission begins with his act of creation and is renewed through his covenant with Noah. Exodus comes later. The covenant with Noah is a *berith 'olam*: a 'covenant for ever' (Gen. 9.11, 16), and, unlike the covenant with Abraham, is a universal covenant inviting the 'whole human race' into a partnership with God. The Christian Church stands within this universal covenant, shares the particularities of the covenant with Abraham and is born out of a new covenant established through the Spirit in Jesus Christ. These three covenants reflect the Trinitarian nature of God: the universal Father; the particularity of the Son; and the recreating power of the Holy Spirit. I am proposing that from a missiological point of view,[11] the covenant with Noah is foundational in that it provides the theological context for the establishment of later covenants.[12]

A universal covenant

The covenant with Noah, according to Karl Barth, is a covenant of grace expressing the free and utterly unmerited self-obligation of God to the whole human race.[13] God promises in this covenant to both preserve and save all the inhabitants of the planet from the 'waters of destruction'. The rainbow is a sign that all are included in God's redemptive activity. Genesis 10, showing the migration of the sons of Noah over the known world (Gen. 10.23), is a theological way of expressing this universal 'rainbow covenant'. Although the Bible concentrates on the faith-story of the Jewish and Christian peoples, it also sets out a parallel tradition showing God at work in and through people other than the Israelites.[14]

The rainbow covenant

There is the story of Abraham's meeting with Melchizedek (Gen. 14.19), Moses' association with Jethro – a priest of Midian (Ex. 18), God's direct revelation to Balaam – the prophet of Moab (Num. 22.35), the goodness of Rahab – the harlot (Josh. 2.4). Neither should we forget the revelatory significance of the books of Job, Ruth and Daniel.[15] There is also the wisdom literature of the Old Testament: that common cultural commodity of Israel and her neighbours.[16] In the New Testament, Jesus refers in an inclusive way to the Queen of Sheba (Matt. 12.42), the people of Nineveh (Lk. 11.29–32), the widow of Zarephath and Naaman the Syrian (Lk. 4.25–6). When beginning his ministry, our Lord probably thought his mission was to be directed only to the lost sheep of the house of Israel. His encounter with the Canaanite woman (Matt. 15.21–8) changed this, for he hears the Father speaking through the voice of an outsider and realizes that he is to be the saviour of the world.[17] Jesus paints a picture of God as the Father of compassion and grace, the God who makes the sun 'rise on the evil and the good and sends rain on the righteous and the unrighteous' (Matt. 5.45). In the rain and sun, rainbows cover the earth.

The Old Testament gives other hints of God's saving activity amongst the nations. In the book of Amos, God says:

Did I not bring up Israel from the land of Egypt, and the Philistines from Caphtor and the Syrians from Kir? (Amos 9.7)

In Isaiah, we learn that God will save and liberate Egypt and bless Assyria just as he has done with Israel:

The Lord will make himself known to the Egyptians; and the Egyptians will know the Lord in that day and worship with sacrifice and burnt offering, and they will make vows to the Lord and perform them . . . In that day Israel will be the third with Egypt and Assyria, a blessing in the midst of the earth, whom the Lord of hosts has blessed, saying,

'Blessed be Egypt my people, and Assyria the work of my hands, and Israel my heritage.' (Isa. 19.21–5)

Not only does God work his salvation among the outsiders but also he chooses them as instruments 'for' salvation. Thus of Cyrus, the Persian, God says:

He is my shepherd and he shall fulfil all my purpose, saying of Jerusalem, 'She shall be built.' (Isa. 44.28)

The story of Jonah shows us another feature of this universal covenant by illustrating that 'it is possible to be at the same time a citizen of Nineveh and a worshipper of Yahweh'.[18]

The word from outside

Karl Barth, in later volumes of his *Church Dogmatics*, became increasingly interested in people outside the Church.[19] By anchoring his theology in God's covenant and expounding his doctrine of creation on the basis of grace, he came to see that creation had become 're-tuned' to the Word of God. This Word, heard first in Jesus Christ, finds a resonance in the external voices of the world. T. F. Torrance answers Barth's puzzled, exclusive followers:

Why should not the Word of God awaken some response and beget some fruit for itself outside the boundaries of the Church, beyond the frontiers of faith, in the world of secular life and culture? . . . Why should not the Church listen to these echoes if only as a mirror of its actual equivocal life, as a challenge to correct its tradition or an impulse to reform?[20]

Jesus Christ is 'the true witness' who actualizes God's salvation in our world. He is the 'light of life'[21] and, because of Noah's covenant of grace, becomes the source of other lights which shine outside the Church.[22] The world, as the 'theatre' of God's glory, possesses a luminosity which comes from the Word of God. No wonder Barth rejoiced in the music of

Mozart and chuckled at the theological embarrassment of his own exclusive followers.[23] More outrageously still, Barth chooses, as an example of 'a true witness', not Paul or Peter, but Job. Job is not only an Old Testament figure; he is also an Edomite, a pagan outsider!

Like Noah's contemporaries, Job faces destruction. Job's words and silences are protests against what he perceives to be a destroying God. His friends are certainly theologically correct in their spelling out of timeless truths.[24] Yet truth about a covenant God has to be incarnated into the tension and struggle of particular historical situations if it is to be real truth. Job is righteous because, unlike his theological comforters, he has been forced by God to abandon everything including his understanding of God. He therefore refuses to engage in dialogue with them. It is not just a meaningless exercise, it has actually become for him an ingredient of satanic assault.[25] The topsy-turvy feature of the book of Job is that when God finally speaks, Job hears him through 'the echo of the voice of creation'.[26] He is not given a theological answer, but rather a lesson in cosmology and zoology with 'its successive pictures of lions and ravens, hippopotamus and crocodile'.[27] It is as if Noah's animals pass before him. Job is being encouraged by God to look more closely at creation and seek his own answers to the angry questions he poses.

An ecological covenant

'Creation is the outward basis of the covenant (Gen. 1) and covenant the inward basis of creation (Gen. 2).'[28] The Bible opens with what has been described as the 'missionary' act of God in creation. This is followed up immediately with God's invitation to share his mission with humanity: [29]

> So God created man in his own image, in the image of God he created him; male and female he created them. God blessed them and said to them, 'Be fruitful and increase in number; fill the earth and subdue it.' (Gen. 1.27–8)

Made in God's image, all women and men become partners with God in an 'ecological mission'.[30] Carol Meyers points to the imaginative interplay between the Hebrew word for 'man', *adam* (which is both male and female), and the stuff from which humankind is formed *adamah*, usually translated 'ground' or 'earth'. It is the fusion of earth and breath which creates all life.[31] It has been suggested that if Adam is the founding father of gardening then Noah is surely the founding father of wildlife conservation (Gen. 9.12).[32]

The entire cosmos, so the Hebrews believed, stood on two pillars: a pillar of justice and a pillar of righteousness (Ps. 97.2).[33] If a crack appeared in either, the ecological system would become unbalanced (Ps. 82). If a serious rupture occurred, then the primal chaotic waters, which in Hebrew mythology were held back by the dome of the heavens and fabric of the earth, would pour in to destroy all life. This is what happened in the flood (Gen. 7.11). God now seeks to restore justice and righteousness to the ecosystem and instructs us to assist him in this priestly task. Mission has to be viewed symbiotically.[34] That is, we as God's co-creators must learn how to relate to each other and to our environment so that the subject–object categories which we currently use to analyse, assess and judge, are transcended by relational categories. This is what one might expect if we are truly made in the image of the triune God of covenant.

Some of us who live in the colder northern climes may find this difficult. A cool theology which divides and separates things is more to our taste. Yet the majority of the world's population habitually go barefoot and expose their bodies to the sun. The peoples of Asia and Africa have a much more integrated understanding of themselves as physical and spiritual beings. They also have an intuitive awareness of earth, mountains, air, water and fire and of the importance of ancestors, dreams and spirits.[35] They feel a relationship with creation which we, as city dwellers in Britain, have largely lost.[36] They more easily understand how Job receives the Word of God in whirlwind, sea and stars (Job 38.1; 16.31). For them, too, the mountain goats, donkeys, oxen, ostriches, horses, hawks, eagles, hippopotamus and crocodile (Job 39; 40; 41) are revelatory.

Our ancestors knew this once. Sadly our Western leisure and work activities have, until recently, tended to exploit rather than protect the planet.[37] The exposing of our bodies to the elements, walking or travelling slowly[38] are not generally features of cool, contemporary Britain. In the 'by-gone' days of the nineteenth century, the upper-middle classes visited the 'far country' as 'travellers', planning their own itineraries and taking time and thought to prepare themselves. Nowadays the tourist industry gets you from A to B as quickly as possible and ensures, for your convenience, that B is very much like A. You are also whisked quickly from one historic site to another so that all you can do is point a camcorder or take a 'snap'. 'Travellers' have now become 'tourists' in this McDonaldiza-tion of the world.[39] In total contrast, the middle-aged Words-worth is reputed to have walked some 180,000 miles, so it is hardly surprising that many of his poems express a mystical relationship with nature.[40] Wordsworth returned to Tintern; Christians return to the rainbow covenant and to Jesus who shows us a God who takes delight in the birds of the air and the lilies in the field (Matt. 6.26f.).

When the universal covenant becomes the foundation for mission, then humankind is called to engage in ecological activity as God seeks to renew his image in humanity.[41] The medley of nations emerging under the rainbow sign must never lose its sense of wonder at God's unlimited grace made manifest through the whole created order for 'in him we live and move and have our being' (Acts 17.28).

The universal mandates

In all covenants there is a 'sending' (mission) action and instructional mandates. In establishing the rainbow covenant God says, 'Go forth from the ark ... Bring forth with you every living thing that is with you'(Gen. 8.16). This is followed by a command to work with the creator in renewing the face of the earth:

> Be fruitful and multiply, and fill the earth. (Gen. 9.1)

> You shall not eat flesh with its life . . . Whoever sheds the blood of man, by man shall his blood be shed; for God made man in his own image. (Gen. 9.4–6)

The first mandate (Gen. 9.1) transports us back to the beginning of Genesis and argues for a repopulation of the earth.[42] Growth is implicit in the mandates given to Adam and Noah. The table of nations in Chapter 10 describes the outworking of a theological process which reaches a climax in Paul's speech on the Areopagus where he argues that 'from one man God made every nation of men, that they should inhabit the whole earth; and that he determined the times set for them and the exact places where they should live' (Acts 17.26).[43] Raymond Panikkar believes growth to be essential to all religions, for 'in the life of a religion as in the life of a person . . . [if] there is no growth, there is deterioration. To stop means stagnation and death.'[44] While the mandate to multiply is biological and geographical, it can by no means exclude the social and religious dimensions of being human (Acts 17.27–8).

Christianity is growing in many parts of the world, but so too are many of the non-Christian faith communities. Because Noah's covenant is universal, this growth should not surprise us. God, however, places limits on numerical growth.[45] In the second mandate (Gen. 9.4–6) there is a prohibition against taking life. 'Human life must be considered as given by God for a specific purpose and set under his special protection, and therefore must be treated with holy awe,' writes Barth in a chapter entitled (following Albert Schweitzer) 'Respect for Life'.[46] John Wesley also spelt out the necessity of treating animals with tenderness and respect, for 'God is the fountain of all the life which man possesses in common with the animals'.[47] The growth of a nation, faith or system is considered legitimate, under this universal covenant, only in as far as it respects the life of other nations, faiths or systems and, in addition, exercises a respectful stewardship of the planet and all its inhabitants. One of David Landes conclusions at the end of his masterly book *The Wealth and Poverty of Nations* is that if the human race is to have a future 'we do have to attend to the serious, progressive, and possible irremediable damage we are inflicting on the environment'.[48] All this has implications for dialogue, development and justice:

> The Christian hope is that God is working for the good of all through all things and that he will bring the new for the benefit of all. Therefore justice, more than ever before, must be justice for all humanity. And justice includes nature as well as humanity.[49]

These two mandates belong together for there can be no genuine growth without respect for one another and no adequate understanding of development if thereby we deny self determination to others. The second mandate puts limits on the first by suggesting that it is not God's purpose that any one people should grow geographically at the expense of another. God wants to give salvation, in the form of 'living space', to all people.[50]

In South Africa the spirit of these mandates is encapsulated in the concept of *ubuntu*.[51] Communality rather than individualism lies at the heart of this idea which is holistic, symbiotic and excludes all Western dualism. *Ubuntu* is a rich 'soul' concept of respect for the earth and for one another. The land is held to be sacred, belonging to the spirits of the past, and therefore cannot be owned by individuals.[52] You do not kill or steal because it will bring misfortune on your family,[53] instead you show other people kindness, courtesy, hospitality and share what you have.[54] The Kenyan-born theologian John Mbiti sums up this idea:

> Only in terms of other people does the individual become conscious of his own being, his duties, his privileges and

responsibilities towards himself and towards other people . . . The individual can only say 'I am because we are; and since we are, therefore I am.' [55]

Life under the rainbow is a life of interdependence. Desmond Tutu explains: 'When I dehumanize you I inexorably dehumanize myself.'[56] This understanding of humanity creates an enormous capacity for forgiveness. Once an African detects that a person means well and can be trusted, there is a readiness to let go of the past and joyfully move into a hopeful future. Nelson Mandela's willingness to forgive and join hands with his oppressors for the transformation of South Africa is an apt illustration of this.[57] This concept of *ubuntu* has continued within the South African Truth and Reconciliation Commission where the aim of passing judgement has been transcended by the necessity of bringing secret pain and terror to the surface. Perpetrators and the victims can now have a future together in the same 'rainbow nation'.[58]

Similar injunctions reflecting these rainbow covenant mandates are found in other cultures and religions. In the New Testament:

So whatever you wish that men would do to you, do so to them; for this is the law and the prophets. (Matt. 7.12)

In the Jewish Talmud:

What is hateful to yourself do not do to your fellow men. That is the whole of the Torah.[59]

In the Muslim Hadith:

No man is a true believer unless he desires for his brother that which he desires for himself.[60]

The Hindu Mahabharata:

One should never do to another that which one would regard as injurious to oneself. This, in brief, is the rule of righteousness.[61]

In the Buddhist Sutta Nipata:

As a mother cares for her son, all her days, so towards all living beings a man's mind should be all embracing.[62]

So communities have to 'go forth' and 'bring forth'. They are to grow, increase, multiply and develop the resources of the earth (Gen. 9.1–3) so that a future for themselves and the planet is assured. This must be balanced by respect for the religion, culture, convictions and self-determination of other people, and a reverence for life in all its diverse forms. Max Warren eloquently sums up this approach to mission:

Our first task in approaching another people, another culture, another religion, is to take off our shoes, for the place we are approaching is holy. Else we may find ourselves treading on men's dreams. More serious still, we may forget that God was here before our arrival.[63]

Second interlude: Saccidananda

I am sitting under the porch of a little hut set amongst the palmyra trees facing the waters of the sacred River Cauvery. Some little boys are attempting to chase a cow. There is much shouting but little movement from the creature. The sun shines down and I sit soaking it up. I feel a great sense of peace all around.

When three days earlier, passing through the archway I saw the words 'Saccidananda Ashram' and glimpsed the assortment of low thatched buildings nestling among the trees, my spirits lifted. I almost wept with relief when the sister led me to this little hut with its whitewashed walls, thatched roof, and four shuttered windows named after the four winds. Standing in its cool simplicity I experienced a sense of benediction. In this 'far country' I had at last come home. I am still weak with the fever which laid me low a week ago. I had felt so lonely and lost despite the kindness of my hosts, who kept visiting me as I lay tossing and sweating in the burning heat at Madurai which surely has some of the most vicious and persistent mosquitoes in India. I now recognized the relentlessness of my itinerary since arriving a month before. My travels, the culture shock, conversations, constant uncertainty, preaching, writing and delivering the Abraham Malpan lectures in the Mar Thoma Church of Kerala followed by my time at Tamil Nadu Theological Seminary in Madurai had all taken their toll.

This morning I woke at dawn and walked beside the silent river. The red glow in the east and the first flashes of light revealed the silhouettes of women bathing and two men driving oxen. The mile-wide river in this season before the monsoon is reduced to a sandy desert through which flow a number of tiny streams teaming with fish. I paddled and splashed feeling my health returning in these sacred waters. With the rapidly increasing light came the unmistakable smell of India, the cry of exotic birds and the tinkle of distant bells. This was the India I had imagined. It was an intoxicating moment.

I had come to see Father Bede Griffiths. I was not alone for even though there were only a few visitors, some of these were formidable. I now avoid a very self-opinionated lady from Oxford, England, and two others from the US. Those from Germany, Holland, France are less intrusive. Most of the visitors, who seem very middle class and like myself pretending to be Indian, catch the spirit of the place and behave with sensitivity and grace. At meal times, we sit in rows on the floor and the food is slopped out into our bowls from buckets. The sisters eat ravenously, I find the food unpalatable. Only the hot sweet tea restores me. For three days I have lived on bananas and give my food to the cow who happily gobbles it up.

I am fascinated by Father Bede. His 'public school' accent

and the saffron robes of the *sannyasi* are strangely incongru-
ous. He has a tall gaunt frame, white hair and a flowing Father
Christmas beard. He possesses great charisma, projects a
warm vitality and there is a youthful twinkle in eyes which are
very beautiful. In his presence you actually feel you are the
most important person in the world. No wonder the Indians
prostrate themselves before him and kiss his feet to honour
this 'holy man'. In my two conversations we talked about the
state of the Western Church, the type of missionary needed for
India, the place of dialogue, the struggle for justice (I disagreed
with him), the nature of the power which resides in the great
Menakshi Temple in Madurai, the validity of miracles (some
Hindu *sannyasi* have the power to raise people from the dead)
and the difference between spiritual and psychic powers.
When I returned weeks later to Saccidananda with my wife
Christine, Father Bede remembered and wanted to see us
both. Christine too received his benediction.

The Eucharist here takes you to the very throne of God. The
rhythmic sound of the *tabalas* and *tamburas* which accom-
pany the Tamil *bhajans* weave mysterious melody through the
celebration. The sense of wonder is accentuated by the profu-
sion of Indian symbols, particularly the light, fire and water.
During the offertory, water is sprinkled around the gifts and
upon us the congregation reminding us of our baptism. Father
Bede conducts the two-hour service with unhurried grace and
gentleness. The bread and wine and the fruits of the earth are
offered to God; flowers are placed around the gifts; incense is
waved, as is the flame of burning camphor. We are led into a
remembrance of the cosmic sacrifice of Christ. This is a Mass
for creation in which we the worshippers are caught up in
God's ecological recreation of all things. All of us receive the
bread and the wine; the rules of Rome are far away.
Something greater is here. The bread, the wine, the smoke, the
burning lamps and the flames of fire transfigure the present.
Eternity is near.

I shall never forget our last evening Eucharist at Saccidananda; the rhythmic beat of the music, the flickering lamps,

our foreheads marked with ash as a sign of our mortality, the words of Father Bede's blessing, our desire to prostrate ourselves in the darkness before God as the inner temple of the 'holy of holies' is shut for the night. Christine and I left the building in darkness to gaze at a sky illuminated by millions of stars and galaxies. Strolling hand in hand by the sacred river we watched the dancing lights of fireflies in the trees above us. While returning to our little hut to listen to the scamper of rodents in the thatching overhead and the sound of frogs croaking in the pool outside, the power and beauty of God overwhelmed us. I realized then that we, like so many others in the Western Church, were suffering from spiritual starvation. How would we cope with the dull diet of Sunday worship when we return to England? We have lived under the rainbow sign. Our lives will never be the same again.

3

From exclusion to embrace

Forgive us the narrowness of vision which sees only the clouds and misses the rainbow. (Thomas à Kempis)

People in the West, said Father Bede, are living with only half a soul, the conscious, rational and masculine part. We must learn how to draw from the unconscious, intuitive and feminine part of our inner being. Bede Griffiths came to India in 1955 seeking a theological marriage between East and West. On his arrival he was struck by this world of immeasurable beauty and vitality, where people lived from the body and not from the ego.

> On all sides was a swarming mass of humanity, children running about quite naked, women in saris, men with turbans, everywhere displaying the beauty of the human form. Whether sitting or standing or walking there was a grace in all their movements and I felt that I was in the presence of a hidden power of nature.[1]

His experience resonated with my own. India, he said, resembled a flower garden of wondrous colours, contrasting smells and sensuality. Despite the poverty and misery, it was a place where one encountered abundant life and spontaneous joy. He spoke of the Indian temples as a replication of the inner spirit, the *Atman*, at whose centre was the formless mysterious divinity often represented by the lingam of bare stone. All life was sacred. Sexuality, unlike our Western preoccupation with sex, was something 'holy'. As a Benedictine in search of God, he felt himself increasingly drawn to live as the poorest of the poor and sought to adopt the life of the *sannyasi*. Although the *sannyasi* is a holy man living solely by faith and totally dependent on the grace gifts of others, through his own self-denial and contemplation, a *sannyasi* has passed beyond any dependence on 'want'.

The marriage of East and West

Vatican II acknowledged the importance of the relationship between faith and culture. It recognized that each human community, as well as having its own specific history and geography, had its particular inheritance of wisdom expressed through and in its own culture.[2] Everyone lives according to some culture, for culture is both a materialization of the human spirit and a spiritualization of matter.[3] Culture shapes us.[4] The *Evangelii Nuntiandi* of Pope Paul VI speaks of the 'evangelization of culture':

> The split between the gospel and culture is without a doubt the drama of our time, just as it was of other times. Therefore every effort must be made to ensure a full evangelization of culture, or more correctly of cultures. They have to be regenerated by an encounter with the gospel.[5]

This missionary process, to which Father Bede responded, is called 'inculturation'. Inculturation has its source in the mystery of the incarnation. Inculturation sees mission as the Word taking the flesh of a particular culture and expressing itself through the images, symbols and thought forms of that culture.[6] Inculturation is not a simple external adaptation of culture for it seeks, in embracing culture, to transform and transcend it.[7] 'True inculturation occurs when the gospel penetrates the heart of the cultural experience and shows how Christ gives new meaning to authentic human values.'[8]

Father Bede's arrival at the Saccidananda Ashram enabled inculturation to be more fully developed. This holy place beside the Cauvery river becomes a sign of the absolute being of God (*sat*), known in pure consciousness (*cit*) and communicating absolute bliss (*ananda*). Father Bede said it was modelled on Taizé. He wished it to be a place of inspiration where people from the West could come and rediscover the wholeness of the faith they had lost. Father Bede, echoing the words of his friend C. S. Lewis,[9] explained that if the Western missionary had come not to establish 'missions' but as single missionaries living in poverty and taking the saffron robes of a *sannyasi*, then all India would have embraced Christianity.

Some ministers and students of the Church of South India were very critical of Father Bede. As former converts from Hinduism, they wanted to establish a clear boundary between Christianity and the all-enveloping inclusiveness of their former faith. Christ was not to be included within the Hindu pantheon of gods. Christian worship must take place in a church building and not in a building designed like a temple. Others believed that Father Bede's philosophy, a product of Western idealism and romanticism, had no place in India. Some people in England see him as a perpetrator of 'new-age' religion. They fail to recognize that his theology springs from his conviction that the whole of creation took place in Christ and that 'all things were created through him and for him . . . and in him all things hold together' (Col. 1.16–17). There is a 'rainbow' Trinitarian foundation to Saccidananda. Father Bede writes:

> As the Father knows himself in the Son, and the Son in the Father, so the Father and Son communicate in the love of the Holy Spirit. The Holy Spirit is this expression of love within the Godhead, the relation of love which unites the persons of the Godhead, and yet there is in it no 'duality' but an identity of nature and consciousness in the bliss of love. Thus the bliss of the Godhead in the Christian view is the overflowing love of God, the mysterious communication of love within the Godhead.[10]

Those most critical of Father Bede are often unaware that

their own version of Christianity has unconsciously absorbed the Western culture of science, materialism, abstraction and dualism. They fail to see the inescapable doubleness of culture both as a source of possible deceptive captivity and as a stimulus for incarnating new expressions of the gospel.[11] In my conversation with the Indian artist, Jyoti Sahi, whose work adorns many Asian churches,[12] I was reminded that in the West we seek truth through 'either/or' rather than 'both/and' categories. He pointed out that 'either/or' models are exclusive while the latter are inclusive. We need to appreciate that it is often the poet and the artist who express the mystery of God in the most imaginative and telling way.[13]

The great commission: journey and presence

It has been said that in the Indian context, a colonial attitude has seriously obscured a proper approach to the 'great commission'.[14] This triumphalist tone can be attenuated if we focus on the twin strands of 'journey' and 'presence'. The Greek word *poreuomai*, means 'to depart, to leave, to cross boundaries' (Matt. 28.7, 19). The word reminds us of the peripatetic Jesus who repeatedly crossed boundaries to reach out under the rainbow sign to all on the periphery.

Diana Eck describes three types of journey.[15] There are first, the outward-bound trips into the unknown. They follow the pattern of Noah's departure from the ark, of Abraham's journey from Haran (Gen. 12.4–9), of Moses' trek across the wilderness, and of Siddhartha Gautama's abandonment of his family at the dead of night. These are journeys of exploration which give birth to religions of liberation. Secondly, there are the home-bound journeys. Here the destination is clearly defined as we travel back to some source of faith. So Muslims go to Mecca, Christians travel to the Holy Land and Hindus return to Benares. Lastly, there are the wanderings. The point of these journeys is not so much to get there, 'there' being largely unknown, but to discover what it means to be 'on the way'. So our Lord tells inquirers that 'foxes have holes, and birds of the air have nests; but the Son of man has nowhere to lay his head' (Matt. 8.20).

These journeys are slow journeys inviting people to become pilgrims, and 'tourists' to become 'travellers'. There are frequent stops along the way. If time, reflection and effort are taken, they can become journeys of revelation. Contemporary Christianity in the West is suffering from two temptations. There is the temptation to move fast, so transforming 'travellers' into 'tourists' thereby reducing a 'pilgrimage' to a 'package'. The other temptation is to journey backwards to some haven of supposed tranquillity. A Church which offers womb-like security more easily attracts those baffled and battered by today's uncertainties. While Matthew's Gospel contains references to all three types of journey, the 'great commission' reverses the backward pilgrimage into a forward journey. On Easter morning the women go back to the place where they had laid Jesus. In the tomb (womb) they are told:

> He is not here; for he has risen, as he said. Come; see the place where he lay. Then go quickly and tell his disciples that he has risen from the dead, and behold, he is going before you to Galilee. (Matt. 28.6–7)

They are then sent on an outward-bound mission to find the Living God in the 'far country'.

In Matthew's Gospel the kingdom is the locus of incarnation and Jesus is the incarnate one. He is 'Immanuel'. In our post-resurrection period 'we can speak of incarnation as mediated through those events and people in which God is present, that is where the *missio Dei* is carried out and fulfilled'.[16] While Jesus affirms the Mosaic *Torah* as having abiding significance (5.17–20), he rejects the Pharisaic development of it.[17] The New Testament scholar John Ziesler, commenting on Matthew 28.20, takes the Jewish statement 'If two sit together and the words of the Law [are spoken] between them, the divine Presence rests between them' to mean that Christ is present in the same way as the glory (*shekinah*) is present with those who meet around the Mosaic *Torah*. Like a princess in rags, God's *shekinah* lies hidden in the material texture of the world waiting to be discovered. Jesus has now become the 'mode of divine presence'.[18] Matthew, through his allusion at the beginning of the Sermon on the Mount to Moses on Sinai (5.1), pictures Jesus as giving a new *Torah*. His theology suggests that disciples come to dwell in the presence of Yahweh (*shekinah*) through keeping this new *Torah* of Jesus. Christian disciples journeying into the unknown and obeying everything Jesus commanded, experience the reality of the rainbow promise, 'I AM with you' (Matt. 28.20).

So Father Bede journeyed to India and while standing before the colossal three-faced figure of Siva Maheswara in the cave of Elephanta near Bombay, suddenly felt overwhelmed by the majesty and mystery (*shekinah*) of the great God.[19] Thomas Merton had a similar experience when visiting the stone carvings of the Buddha at Polonnaruwa. The great 'I AM' chooses to reveal himself to us when we journey and respond to his commands.

The rise and fall of the rainbow dream

Father Bede's journey to India and his programme of inculturation raises the question of where one draws the line between faith and culture. Many of the modern charismatic churches in India, established and financed by American missionaries, simply attempt to replicate their own US versions of Christianity, the religious equivalent of McDonald's. I was told with wry humour that many Hindus converted in order to enjoy Western benefits but secretly continued going to the Hindu temples. The Saccidananda Ashram was for me an inclusive sign of the rainbow covenant in a country littered with former imperial expressions of a defunct Western dream. One of my most depressing moments in India was preaching in a decaying Victorian building. We sang unaccompanied from *Hymns Ancient and Modern*. The pipe organ stood in the side transept covered in grime, its mechanisms long since consumed by rodents and humidity. The small congregation, so bright and lively outside the building, sat unresponsive, motionless and far away. The stately liturgy of Cranmer reflected an England of long ago imposed by Empire. I kept asking myself how did we get to this?

In the last two hundred years the industrial revolution enabled the European nations to try to realize their own version of the rainbow dream. The nineteenth-century missionary rode on the back of this economic and technological imperialism. Enthusiastic missionaries fired by the gospel, went to the ends of the earth 'seeking souls' who they believed were 'lost' in darkness. It was a heroic time of expansion and evangelical passion:

> Far, far away in heathen darkness dwelling,
> Millions of souls for ever may be lost;
> Who, who will go, salvation's story telling,
> Looking to Jesus, minding not the cost?[20]

The music of this rainbow vision was reflected in the Edinburgh Missionary Conference of 1910. At this world gathering, inspired by the euphoria of the expansive West,[21] the missionaries present set their target: the evangelization of the world in one generation. There have been similar calls ever since, for the dream lives on. But this left-over of nineteenth-century optimism was to be shattered. In 1914 an incident in a tiny Balkan state sent shock waves rippling first across Europe and subsequently across the world. One by one nations were sucked into a terrifying encounter. Within a couple of years all the peoples of the earth had become caught up in a holocaust of destruction. Here indeed was a nightmare response to the missionary dream. The Christian West instead of being the propagator of light became a creator of hell on earth. This was the beginning of the end for Europe, for it had lost its Christian credibility. The drift of people from the churches became a veritable stampede. William Fullerton's hymn is bereft of former confidence:

I cannot tell how he will win the nations,
How he will claim his earthly heritage,
How satisfy the needs and aspirations
Of east and west, of sinner and of sage. [22]

Europe's time had passed. In the thirteenth and fourteenth centuries the expanding edges of the Old European World had been divided up by Venice and Genoa. In the wake of more far-reaching voyages of exploration in the first half of the fifteenth century and the discovery of the New World, Spain and Portugal staked their competing claims. In the eighteenth and nineteenth centuries the powerful nations of France and Britain moved to centre stage and fought for global supremacy. After the great depression and the Hitler madness two new super-giants, the United States of America and the Soviet Union, stalked the earth bearing hideous weapons. Their antagonism became a sort of frozen paranoia. Yet the paralysis of the mighty gave the small peoples their chance. They who had passively been drawn into the wars of the rich, not unnaturally wanted to eat from the rich man's table. In the cold post-war climate new nations started to emerge. In a world which had contracted into a global village, those who had fought for the Western allies now wanted their own autonomy.

Before these momentous events many Western churches lost their nerve. As we in Britain entered the sixties period when materially we 'never had it so good', many social and religious prophets, aware of the potential of technology and the decline of the churches, were predicting the end of religion itself. The world was coming of age. Harvey Cox begins his book *The Secular City* with the words, 'The rise of urban civilization and the collapse of traditional religion are the two hallmarks of our era and are closely related movements.'[25] Callum Brown in his book *The Death of Christian Britain* argues that the sixties marked a significant collapse of the British churches and concludes that what was taking place 'was not merely the continuing decline of organized Christianity but the death of the culture which formerly conferred

Christian identity upon the British people as a whole'.[24] His book ends with the depressing statement: 'Britain is showing the world how religion as we have known it can die.'[25]

The new barbarians

Of the old gospel, there was now little left to proclaim. The plug had been pulled on the 1910 world missionary enterprise. The watershed came in the Fourth Assembly of the World Council of Churches. The year was 1968, the same year that Father Bede came to the Cauvery river. At its meeting in Uppsala it was publicly acknowledged that the old dream had died. Confidence in technology's secular vision was questioned as scientist and engineer struggled to manage the machines and structures they had created. A clash appeared at Uppsala between those who advocated a humanization programme and the evangelicals who saw the mission of God in terms of evangelization. It was, in Hoekstra's phrase, the 'eclipse of evangelism'.[26] The tide of institutional Christianity was not only ebbing but Western culture itself had been poisoned and traumatized by the genocides and war machines of the twentieth century.[27] Our world has become scarred by exclusions and cries out for healing through embrace.

The mood in 1980 at the Ninth World Conference on Mission and Evangelism in Melbourne was apocalyptic. The world of the twentieth century had become a far more horrifying place than they had imagined. A simple ecclesiastical formula joining evangelism and social responsibility would not suffice:

> We meet under the clouds of nuclear threat and annihilation. Our world is deeply wounded by the oppressions inflicted by the powerful upon the powerless. These oppressions are found in our economic, political, racial, sexual and religious life. Our world, so proud of human achievements, is full of people suffering from hunger, poverty and injustice.[28]

Alasdair MacIntyre in his important book *After Virtue*,[29] draws a parallel between the twentieth-century world of Europe and North America and the epoch in which the Roman Empire declined into the Dark Ages:

> For some time now we too have reached that turning point. What matters at this stage is the construction of local forms of community within which civility and the intellectual and moral life can be sustained through the new dark ages which are already upon us. And if the tradition of the virtues was able to survive the horrors of the last dark ages, we are not entirely without grounds for hope. This time, however, the barbarians are not waiting beyond the frontiers; they have already been governing us for some time.

He reaches this conclusion by arguing that contemporary governments create 'institutional arrangements for imposing a bureaucratic unity'. MacIntyre recognized that most liberals will dispute this as they believe a multiplicity of visions is possible. Socialists too would have disagreed, maintaining the dominant world-view to be Marxist. But, says MacIntyre, both of these positions arise from the collapse of the central ground. Marxism and liberalism fail because their core is deeply optimistic. Human nature is tarnished and sinful. The world's future is threatened when governments relentlessly pursue their own chosen brand of ideology. Our problems arise because governments have lost the notion of 'general good'. Modern politics is civil war carried on by other means. It is therefore essential for us in this age of barbarism to guard the few common virtues that remain. In introducing his later book, *Three Rival Versions of Moral Enquiry*, he is even more pessimistic and doubts whether the memory of virtues can hold back the encroaching chaos.[30]

Although many will not accept MacIntyre's gloomy analysis, he does steer a course which tries to make intellectual sense of the present age, while at the same time rejecting the despair of ideological fundamentalism and the vacuousness of relativism. Nicholas Lash in his book *Theology on the Way to Emmaus*, having considered MacIntyre's analysis, suggests that the mission of the Church is to establish 'trans-cultural, global networks of local communities, which, in that act and process of remembrance, sustain an absolute hope for all humanity'.[31] This would seem to be an essential task and one which gives contemporary substance to the mission mandates of the rainbow covenant. The Saccidananda Ashram is but one illustration of this.

These 'trans-cultural, global networks' of Church will increasingly find themselves questioning the pervasive culture arising from the effects of 'globalization'.[32] Globalization means different things to different people.[33] It is popularly regarded as the relentless expansion of Western (usually meaning United States) power and influence across the globe. In this book I use the word to describe the transforming processes which are reshaping all patterns of living in every place. Driven mainly by the global financial markets, these processes are impacting on every culture and eroding traditional values. The global financial markets have themselves been likened to a huge juggernaut careering down a mountain out of control.[34] The Church may find herself in the path of this runaway monstrosity.

The fragile rainbow hanging in the sky has to be seen against these threatening thunder clouds of the flood. There is no way back to the garden of Eden, so while human beings pursue the rainbow dream they do so bearing the mark of Cain. While an impressive product of dialogue, the Babel story (Gen. 11.3f.) following hard on the heels of Noah's inclusive covenant conceals the desire to usurp God by creating new gods to ameliorate despair. In the contemporary Western world 'grand ideologies' have now been replaced by the 'soft ideologies' of the free market, the American way or New Age utopianism.[35] The world-wide televized images of smoke over Manhattan on 11 September 2001 and the collapse of the twin towers of the World Trade Center were traumatic revelations of the negative side of globalization. The US fantasy of permanent safety and security was blown apart as they experienced briefly what is the daily lot of 'people in other parts of the world, living under the threat of bombardment and random death'.[36] In the Freudian imagery of towers destroyed by jet aircraft, the clashing symbols of power and freedom, we are given a wake-up call to the danger of exclusive ideologies and the hubris of global capitalism:

> Politically and historically, the twentieth century has manifested the demonic. The dialectical cycle of ambition, pride, inglorious fall, ravaging emptiness and despair, followed by even more extravagant pride and even more total destruction . . . appears and reappears, not as much in myth as in historical actuality. And each step on the cycle repeats itself, as a mirror image . . . In the absence of God, our self-transcending finitude, our temporal creatureliness manifests itself as demonic, lustful and self-destructive, as self-elevation that oppresses others, as desire that devours all else, and as a non-being oppressed by fate and lacerated with emptiness.[37]

As war drums have beaten over Iraq and the Middle East, it would seem that the twenty-first century will perpetuate this same destructive cycle.

A covenant of pain-love

The covenant God of grace is the God of inculturation, incarnation and condescension. In Christ he abandons the 'form of God' and goes into the 'far country'. He chooses, as God, to enter into self-limitation yet at the same time is the Lord of glory.[38] To overcome exclusion God has to limit himself so that we can become his covenant partners and journey with him into the 'far country'.

Noah seeing the rainbow sign above the desolate landscape knew that a new relationship had been established between

God and his recalcitrant partner. Under the rainbow, God engages in mission with his people to prevent a reoccurrence of holocaust. The Hebrew word *qesheth*, 'bow of war', occurs many times in the Old Testament but it is used only here and in Ezekiel 1.28 to describe the 'rainbow'. This sign can be taken to mean that God will never again loose his bow against the world and reduce it to chaos. But the war bow now points upwards, as it were, into the heart of God. Could this mean that if the bolt is fired again not only will creation perish but also God himself will die? Is it a sign, as the Asian theologian Choan-Seng Song suggests,[39] of God's 'pain-love for humanity' reaching its most agonizing depth? If so, then mission is crucial to the very life and future of God. In the covenant, God is risking all in his partnership with us. The purpose of mission is not simply 'humanization', or 'evangelization', neither is it only about the salvation of humankind and the created order. Ultimately the purpose of mission is nothing less than the liberation of God.

Why does God take such a risk? The only possible answer is that God's love is so profound that he takes ultimate responsibility for the very existence of pain in the world. Speaking of the enigma of evil and suffering, Camus may not be too far from the truth when he says, 'man is not entirely to blame; it was not he who started history'.[40]

How can this be? From our point of view, there are a number of possibilities. In a book which explores a selection of theodicies, John Roth argues that God must bear his share of the responsibility for the existence of evil because 'he is the one who ultimately sets the boundaries in which we live and move and have our being'.[41] In the very act of creating the universe, God's sacrificial self-limitation is necessary in the bestowal of his gift of freedom upon creation.[42] Yet what if God's self-restraint is excessive, permitting the emergence of the wild and unrestrained? Second, the first creation story assumes the presence of the wild watery forces of chaos which were later to flood the earth (Gen. 1.1). Although tamed 'they never lose their unpredictable power to upset the order and harmony of creation'.[43] Indeed it has been suggested that chaos exists because of the failure of God's previous attempts at creating.[44] Mess and creativity belong together as any imaginative artist will tell you.[45] But what is the nature of 'the mess' out of which God creates? How toxic is it? A third way of looking at this puzzle is to imagine God creating in the youthful exuberance of play,[46] but such are the explosive energies of Spirit that the chaotic is released alongside the symbiotic. However one tries to explained it, there is tragedy here! Wheat and tares are mysteriously sown into the very structure of this violent universe[47] in such proportions that evil is able to thrive more rapidly than goodness.

Yet this assignment of evil to God's creation is contradicted by the biblical refrain, 'and God saw that it was good' (Gen. 1). I suggest that theodicies of protest are essential in such a world as ours, and the Bible is not devoid of these as illustrated by the book of Job. Indeed, in the face of the covenant-making God, it is faithful human action to rage and protest, since rage is the gate to hope.[48] It is not that God has a moral defect.[49] It is not that God has done an inadequate job. It is a question of whether we can trust such a God who, from our point of view, does not seem to have created what philosophical theology calls 'the best of all possible worlds'.

The rainbow covenant is a sign of God's 'repentance as well as his promise'.[50] God in his grace 'chooses' to hold himself accountable for the tragedies of creation. He does not wish to exclude himself or excuse himself from responsibility. For love's sake he embraces even the failed responsibility of human beings. He becomes the Judge who is Judged in our place.[51] 'He makes his own the being of man under the curse of contradiction, but in order to do away with it as He suffers it. He acts as Lord over this contradiction even as He subjects Himself to it.'[52] The cross, according to Moltmann, is the division of God from God to the utmost degree, while the resurrection is the union of God with God in the most intimate fellowship.[53] So the optimism of grace is revealed in the 'pain-love' of God. It is because he freely and graciously takes to himself the ultimate responsibility for everything that we can say with Job, 'Though he slay me yet will I trust him' (Job 13.15).

So in recurrent acts of grace God scatters sparks of 'his shattered divinity'[54] into the emptiness and leaves living echoes of himself embedded in the moving matrix of history. Yet God is not like the entropic Humpty Dumpty of the Western nursery rhyme, always flying apart in a great measure of disorder. God is not split off from himself; that is our condition. Rather we are witnessing here the pain-love of God for, in the words of Helmut Gollwitzer, 'God himself is forsaken by God, God himself rejects himself'.[55] So creation becomes for God a moment of acute self-awareness and discovery. Good and evil have come to exist in the world and God makes himself accountable and forges a covenant with Noah. By this action he reveals his heart of grace and through the covenant he embraces our flawed existence. It is as if 'God must, therefore, pass through time to attain his own eternal being and in this passage he must experience the pain as un-transmuted pain. Only thus can he transmute it, and, by it, attain his own perfect bliss'.[56] So he 'comes down' (Gen. 11.5) into the 'far country' to experience the pain of a partnership with his violent creation fully. He embraces us along with the brutality of our sin, and it hurts him. Bound to us by his covenant promise God awaits his own liberation in our release. When this is accomplished creation will again dance for joy (Rom. 8.20–1) and God will be able to return from the 'far country'.

In anguish of heart and purpose he now moves through space and time. His mission and our mission are locked together. His own suffering love lures us on. His future and ours is at stake. The redemption of all things is the end, miracles of grace are the means. The music that propels God into mission is not the tooting of heavenly trumpets but the sound of his own primal earth-creating cry of pain.

4

A particular covenant

Go from your country and your kindred and your father's house to the land that I will show you. And I will make you a great nation, and I will bless you, and make your name great, so that you will be a blessing. I will bless those who bless you, and him who curses you I will curse; and by you all the families of the earth shall bless themselves (Gen. 12.1).

Some readers will find this chapter difficult because it deals with the theological idea of election. Can I encourage you to persevere, for election is central to a proper understanding of mission and covenant. You will be pleased to hear that subsequent chapters are much easier to follow.

The first theological ingredient of covenant is 'grace', the second is 'election'. The Trinitarian God wishes to call people into a partnership with himself. God is gracious enough not to be God without humanity. This decision is not arbitrary, it is a decision made within the Godhead before the foundation of the world (Eph. 1.4).

Election and its related doctrine of predestination suggest that God chooses some people and rejects others. This Calvinist interpretation is inappropriate here, for it undermines the very possibility of our being free active partners with God. Election within the Bible is a theological concept which proclaims the grace, love and condescension of God while protecting the mystery and holiness of God. 'The concept of election means that grace is truly grace.'[1] Its basis never lies in the one who is chosen but exclusively in the One who chooses.[2] The choosing within the Trinity is in Jesus Christ who is both elected and elects.[3]

Praise be to the God and Father of our Lord Jesus Christ, who has blessed us in the heavenly realms with every spiritual blessing in Christ. For he chose us in him before the creation of the world to be holy and blameless in his sight. In love he predestined us to be adopted as his sons through Jesus Christ, in accordance with his pleasure and will – to the praise of his glorious grace, which he has freely given us in the One he loves. (Eph. 1.3–6)

This passage is a liturgy of glory, grace and gratitude. God freely chooses us for the purpose of blessing us. In Jesus Christ, and through the Spirit, we are given the gift of freedom to live lives of 'happiness and holiness' (2 Cor. 3.17). From our discussions in the last chapter it should be painfully obvious that, for all our talk of 'freedom', we remain trapped in cages of mammon, living under the threat of catastrophes of our own making and largely unaware of the seriousness of our condition. We spin illusions of freedom not realizing that we have squandered the true freedom which belongs to children of God. Like the lost son in the 'far country', God calls us to 'come to our senses' (Lk. 15.17). God has chosen the process of election to give us back the freedom we have lost.[4]

The Ephesians passage reminds us that our election is 'in Christ'. Because of God's rainbow covenant, all humanity is elect in him. As we saw in Chapter 2, God in Christ seeks to call every member of the human race. It is not a case that some are elect to salvation and others to damnation[5] or that God invites some and not others; rather all are called, both those who are near and those in the 'far country' (Eph. 2.11–13). Election in Christ Jesus is the process whereby God calls a particular person or persons and holds them accountable for calling others.

Because God makes himself responsible for persons, each elect person is made responsible for other persons.[6] The God of covenant partnerships invites particular persons to establish partnerships with other human beings. The aim is community.[7] Election thus understood, when strung out across geographical distance and time, means that not all can be called at the same moment or necessarily in the same way. God uses the geographical ebb and flow of peoples across the face of the earth and through history as the theatre for his electing process. The establishment of networks of communication, mutual responsibility and partnership across space and time are his intended purpose. Through these relationships God seeks to reveal not only our vocation but also his essential nature as love.

The one for the many

Universal holocaust was the context of the first covenant; the cataclysm of Babel provides the context for a new particular covenant.[8] Babel marks the moment when 'the whole primeval history breaks off in shrill dissonance',[9] producing fragmented communities and migrating travellers. From one story we now have to deal with a multitude of parallel stories:

> God is God of all humanity, but between Babel and the end of days no single faith is the faith of all humanity.[10]

> God, the creator of humanity, having made a covenant with all humanity, then turns to one people and commands it to be different in order to teach humanity the dignity of difference . . . Biblical monotheism is not the idea that there is one God and therefore one truth, one faith, one way of life . . . it is the idea that unity creates diversity.[11]

To bring clarity to a confused situation, the one God who is at work in separate histories now invites us to look at the way in which he operates in 'one' history. As a team of 11 football players are selected by the manager to delight a crowd of thousands, so Israel is elected to bring glory to the world. But they are chosen – and here is the irony, as we shall see later in this chapter – not because they are 'winners', but because they are 'losers'! So God in electing Abraham puts the spotlight on one people for the sake of all peoples (Gen. 12.1f).[12] God's election of Israel is important because she was called to be 'a symbol of how God would deal redemptively with every nation . . . In the light of the experience unique to Israel, other nations would learn how their histories can be interpreted redemptively.'[13]

Because God is Trinity, election in the Old Testament is still the Father's election in Christ through the Spirit. Paul in Romans 9 to 11 traces this process of election through Abraham's offspring (Rom. 9.7–14):

> To be chosen, to be elect, therefore does not mean that the elect are the saved and the rest are the lost. To be elect in Christ Jesus, and there is no other election, means to be incorporated into his mission to the world, to be the bearer of God's saving purpose for his whole world, to be the sign and the agent and the first-fruit of his blessed kingdom which is for all. It means therefore, as the New Testament makes abundantly clear, to take our share in his sufferings, to bear the scars of the passion.[14]

The Western missionary enterprise has traditionally begun with Abraham. It has been argued that Israel's relationship with the other nations is centripetal; it pulls them in.[15] Jerusalem is the focus to which the peoples of the earth will come, drawn by the magnetic power of the worship of Yahweh (Isa. 2.2; Zech. 8.23). This vision is supposedly taken over in the New Testament (Matt. 8.11f.) and adopted by Jesus. With the death and resurrection of Christ, the movement becomes centrifugal and moves out. The disciples are sent to the ends of the earth in a progressive expansion of the one to the many. The path leads from tower, through tongues to throne.[16]

There is, however, a major problem here. In starting with one selected and elected 'people of God', other races are turned into 'objects' rather than 'subjects' of history. This ethnological approach can be used to support racism.[17] 'History', writes the Asian theologian Choan-Seng Song, 'cannot be explained by the centrism of Israel.' Walter Brueggemann in his reflections on Amos 9.7 says that the prophet seeks to deny Israel's monopolistic claim that she is 'the only exodus subject of the only exodus event by the only exodus God'.[19] The exodus event of Israel is set in motion not because they are believers but 'because they hurt'.[20] The heart of election for the gracious God of covenant is not the faith of people but the pain of people. It is pain that moves the pain-love of God to embrace those who suffer.

A particular covenant

In the rainbow sign God, to all intents and purposes, places a weapon in our hands which can be thrust up to create a mortal wound in his side. In this second covenant God offers a different sign, but one no less painful. Genesis 15.9–21 tells the story. A mysterious ceremony is enacted with a heifer, goat, ram and two birds. The animals are halved and life-blood spilt while symbolic powers swoop upon the remains.[21] This is not a simple sacrifice since the pieces of meat are neither burned nor eaten. With the sinking of the sun Abraham experiences a 'numinous dread' as God, like a burning fire, moves between the severed pieces. There is no attempt to explain these bizarre events. They witness to something dark and terrifying as God 'cuts' (concludes) a covenant with Abraham. This covenant, forged in the furnace,[22] produces promises which punctuate history. The promise of land is re-iterated, but it is now made clear to Abraham that he himself will not possess it.[23] He is to be spared the turbulent future which awaits his descendants. We are given glimpses of Israel's future of humiliation and exaltation. Genesis 15 describes the gracious covenant as promise; the obligations are spelt out in other passages.

The first presenting obligation is that of circumcision (Gen. 17.9–11). This is a sign, like Noah's rainbow, to help God 'remember' his covenant with Abraham.[24] This painful 'cut' of circumcision is certainly an identity mark for the Israelites.

The uncircumcised person will find himself 'cut off' from his kinsmen.[25] Eight days after the birth of his son, Abraham fulfils his side of the covenant by circumcising Isaac 'as God commanded him' (Gen. 21.4). The apostle Paul takes this sign of obedience and refashions it in the light of Jesus Christ. The new circumcision is of the heart (Rom. 2.29) and the Christian symbol is baptism (Col. 2.11–12).[26]

The other obligation relates to God's Word and Abraham's response to it. As Brueggemann reminds us, 'covenant does not happen in silence'.[27] God commands Abraham to go forth on an exodus journey (Gen. 12.1). There is the call to believe which was reckoned as righteousness (Gen. 15.6) and there is the command to sacrifice his only son (Gen. 22.2). We are not yet into *Torah*, but we are into acts of obedience which give 'shape and purpose and perspective' to Abraham as a partner in the covenant relationship.[28] Abraham teaches us faith. We have here in the Old Testament the two obligations of election which in the 'great commission' become the mandates of baptism and teaching.

Israel's vocation of grace and gratitude

'The central motif in the mission of the people of Israel is their freedom from bondage in Egypt.'[29] God, in choosing Israel, expects them to express grace and gratitude so that all nations can be blessed (Deut. 5.15). Her survival now depends on honouring the oath to do 'good' towards Yahweh.[30] This is not easy for she quickly becomes caught in a series of tensions; the same tensions which have reappeared frequently in the history of the Christian Church. Thomas Thangaraj lists these. There is the tension between religious rituals and the exercise of justice, the tension between ethnic nationalism and liberative universalism, and the tension between understanding mission as either conquest or suffering.[31]

The presence of people already dwelling in the promised land raises a difficult theological problem. These inhabitants are also partners with God, living as they do under the rainbow sign of the first covenant. Surely God is pledged to preserve and give them space, not annihilate them? Is there not a dialectical tension between the first universal covenant and this second particular covenant? Should an adversarial pre-emptive strike be launched against them (Josh. 8.25) or should the option of a peaceful mission of co-existence be tried (Judg. 1.29)? The acuteness of this moral dilemma is brought out by the Jewish scholar Samuel Sandmel:

> It is clear that the promised land had once belonged to others . . . yet they were to lose the land and the Hebrews to gain it. Is there not a certain uneasiness reflected in some of the overtones of Scripture about one people taking a land which had not been theirs?[32]

When the promised land is first mentioned in Genesis 12.1–3, we are told that the Canaanites dwelt there (v. 6). The description 'Canaanite' is a pejorative word for 'anti-covenantal' or as we would say 'anti-neighbourly'.[33] Walter Brueggemann suggests that the book of Deuteronomy sets out a covenantal alternative to the Canaanite way of living. While the writer, speaking through the mouth of Moses, regards the Canaanite lifestyle as a threat he also wants to believe that their exploitive social order can be transformed from within. The sacrificial laws of the Old Testament were designed to ensure that God is acknowledged as the gracious giver of everything to everyone. This is most vividly expressed in the law code of Deuteronomy. The offering of sacrifices often occurs in the context of feasting. To those feasts were invited not only the immediate family but also 'the stranger, the orphan and the widow' (Deut. 12.11f.; 14.28f.).[34] Deuteronomy offers the social alternative of charity and compassion so that the 'haves' and the 'have-nots' can share a common destiny.[35] The vision is one of peaceful coexistence in which poverty is eradicated, boundary markers respected (19.14) and where, even in times of war, little damage is done to the natural environment (20.19–20).[36] Is this vision attempting to overcome the tension between the universal rainbow covenant and the particular covenant with Israel? Joshua offers Israel a choice: 'life' or 'death' (Josh. 24.20). Israel forgets and stumbles into death for:

> the land, source of life, has within it seductive power. It invites Israel to enter life apart from the covenant, to reduce covenant place with all its demands and possibilities to serene space apart from history, without contingency, without demand, without mystery.[37]

The promised land is lost. Israel has come full circle having succumbed to the diseases of Egypt.[38] The consequence is exile. So Israel's special mission of gratitude and doing 'good' grinds to a halt. She is no different from other nations, yet because of God's covenant promise, exile is not the end. Her particular destiny was to be a counter-cultural community giving expression to grace and gratitude. To achieve this she must resist the totalizing threat of world powers like Egypt, Assyria, Babylon and Persia. Her ethic of resistance is sustained by a liturgical memory which revives the reality of covenant.[39]

Israel, bearing the painful mark of circumcision and the promise of a future kingdom, is called to be 'the' sign which accurately reflects God's saving grace as he moves through space and time. God's poignant relationship with Israel also discloses the pain-love and vulnerability of grace. 'Pain voiced and processed is the stuff of this new relationship.'[40] Israel's 'practice of lament' is therefore not marginal but becomes fundamental to her vocation and existence.[41] As she journeys God 'goes himself to his people, he suffers with their suffering, he goes with them into the misery of the foreign land, he wanders with their wanderings'.[42]

True mutuality in the covenant partnership exists when an oppressed people lament and turn in hope to the 'crucified God' and where the vulnerable God embraces the bleeding people. Israel's long settlement in the promised land warped her understanding of covenant partnership. The relationship between God and Israel, although at times strained to breaking point, is held together by a mutuality of waiting. Israel waits for the Lord (Ps. 40.1, 130.5; Isa. 40.31), while the Lord waits for Israel to return (Isa. 44.22; Jer. 4.1; Hos.14.1; Mal. 3.7). Return where? To the place of brokenness and 'hurt' where God first elected them in love. 'Strangely enough, colossal losses reduce Israel to the very condition necessary in God's eyes for election and covenant; a helpless, enslaved people.'[43]

Israel and the Church

Abraham's descendants are called to leave 'God's footprints' across history so that all people might know what this gracious God of covenant is like and step into his shoes. It was a bold plan. But it failed. Israel ceased to reflect his grace and glory because they acted unjustly towards the stranger and the poor. Intoxicated by the land, they settled down and exchanged their God-given vocation as servant for one of mastery and power.[44] Israel succumbed to all the temptations inherent in the three tensions described by Thomas Tangaraj at the start of our last section. Their actions expose the suffering-love of God.[45]

Israel blocked the story. God has to take drastic measures. His room for manoeuvre is small. He has bound himself to the Jews and cannot abandon them, yet they no longer reflect his nature. What is he to do? God's dilemma is encapsulated in two missionary parables found in Matthew's Gospel. The parable of the 'wicked tenants' (Matt. 21.33–43) is a story about human accountability and occupies a pivotal place in Matthew's theology of mission.[46] In graphic sentences Israel's apostasy is described. We also glimpse God's growing anguish as he sends a succession of prophetic messengers, all of whom become victims of Israel's arrogance. The other story, the parable of the 'great feast' (Matt. 22.2–10), is about a divine initiative which arises because of Israel's unworthiness:

The king was angry, and he sent his troops and destroyed those murderers [Jews] and burned their city [Jerusalem]. Then he said to his servants, 'The wedding is ready, but those invited were not worthy. Go therefore to the thoroughfares, and invite to the marriage feast as many as you find.' And those servants went out into the streets and gathered all whom they found, both bad and good; so the wedding hall was filled with guests. (vv. 7–10)

God invites a new people to become inheritors of Abraham's mission (1 Pet. 2.1–10). This new 'particular' people, scattered across the face of the earth, made up of Jews and non-Jews, will have the mandates of Abraham and Noah imprinted on their hearts by the Holy Spirit (Ezek. 36.24–29; Jer. 31.31–34).

We should not drive a wedge between Jews and Christians. Although Jesus Christ, like Adam, represents humankind in general he also represents Israel in particular. God's election of Israel and Israel's obedient response to God is seen to take place in Jesus Christ. Indeed such is the identification that Jesus 'is' Israel. Karl Barth, in his stand against Hitler's programme of antisemitism, argues that our Lord's 'flesh' is 'Jewish flesh'.[47] Jesus Christ's own story resonates with Israel's saga of estrangement and lostness:

He exists as one of these Old Testament men. He does not suffer any suffering, but their suffering; the suffering of the children chastised by their Father. He does not suffer any death, but the death to which the history of Israel moves relentlessly forward. He is silent where Job too had to be silent before God.[48]

Israel failed to read her own story in the life of Jesus, while the Church ironically did not recognize in the Jewish people's rejection of Jesus a monotheistic expression of faith in the very same God that Christians worshipped. But this continuity goes deeper. Both Jews and Christians, believing in the covenant promise to Abraham, look to a day of redemption when history will be broken open and creation restored. However, while sharing this eschatological vision, they disagree in their understanding of the process of redemption. For the Jew redemption takes place 'at the end of history'; for the Christian redemption has already begun to take place 'in history' and will be consummated at the end (Rom. 8.22–3). Both faiths are sustained by this hope. God has not repudiated his covenant with Abraham's descendants. When Disraeli was asked by Queen Victoria what, in his opinion, is a real proof of the existence of God he replied, 'Oh, the Jews, your Majesty.'[49]

Although called by God to evangelize the Gentiles, Paul never forgets his responsibility to the Jews. It has been suggested that Paul, as a Jew, believed himself commissioned to bring the Gentiles to the holy city of Jerusalem and does so when he brings Trophimus, the Ephesian, to Jerusalem (Acts 21.29):

> The visit is nothing less than a sign of the Gentiles' eschatological thank-offering and the nations' pilgrimage to Zion, but it is only a sign, for it is not the earthly Jerusalem, but the Jerusalem above, to which the eschatological people of God belong. It is therefore not the temple, but the band of the 'poor' living there in the still unbelieving Israel, that is the object of the thank-offering.[50]

It can be argued from Romans 9–11 that Paul's missionary venture to the Gentiles is God's round-about way of bringing Israel back to the point where she is able, at last, to fulfill her God-given destiny of blessing all the nations (Rom. 11.11).[51] The descendants of Abraham are chosen by God for special service and are assured of their place in the covenant hope.[52] Israel must fulfil her destiny if God is to be all-in-all (Rom. 11.29–36).

The renewal and restoration of all things will come about through the complementary vocations of each. The Church has not replaced Israel. Once Israel's vocation served as a pre-messianic preparation for the Church. Now the Church's vocation is to be a pre-messianic preparation for Israel. Both bear witness to a gracious God who keeps covenant with Abraham's descendants. The disclosure, on the day of redemption, of the identity of God's particular people will, I suspect, be a total surprise to both Jews and Christians (Matt. 24.30–31).

The particular mandates

The missionary mandates given to Abraham and his descendants in the second covenant do not contradict the mandates given to Noah in the first. They rather reinterpret and deepen them. Abraham is required:

To trust God's promise, let go of the familiar and go out into the unknown (Gen. 12.1).
To demonstrate, through his vocation of sacrificial obedience, the grace and the pain-love of God (Gen. 21.4, 22.2).

Yet before Abraham 'believed' (Gen. 15.6) he was ordered to 'go forth'. If the families of the earth were to be blessed, Abraham had first to step out from the culture, traditions and network of relationships in which he was enmeshed.[53] He leaves his homeland and journeys into the 'far country'. It is a radical departure, possible only because he believes God's promise. His exit, unlike that of the so-called illegal immigrants, is not motivated by bad conditions in the land of his ancestors; Abraham becomes an immigrant because God calls him to be one. He and his descendants are to live among strangers in a foreign land, even a land of exile. In order to portray the grace and pain-love of God, Abraham's descendants have to resist the triumphal worldly powers and the cultures of mammon. This elect community, whether old Israel or the New Testament Christian community, must refuse to 'go with the flow':

You are a chosen people, a royal priesthood, a holy nation, a people belonging to God, that you may declare the praises of him who called you out of darkness into his wonderful light. Once you were not a people, but now you are the people of God; once you had not received mercy, but now you have received mercy. (1 Pet. 2.9–10)

Orlando Costas says that in the Old Testament the Jewish temple was the focus of worship. However, with Christ's death the holy of holies is opened up (Matt. 27.50–1) so that God is revealed and worshipped 'outside the gate'. The focus of revelation has moved from the centre to the edge.[54] God has not replaced one fixed point for another, rather he has established a permanent 'moving centre at the periphery of life'.[55]

This community is given the title 'Church', which translates the Greek word *ecclesia* meaning 'called out'. It suggests a model of Church as 'a community in exile'.[56] It will, by its very nature, only attract those people who, like Abraham, are prepared to live a life of 'radical obedience'. Such a calling must be sustained by 'dangerous memories and dangerous hopes'.[57] This moving counter-cultural ecclesial community has renounced power and glory and embraces the way of the cross. It is a community which knows how to flourish in the 'far country'. Peter Hodgson, in his own description of Church, sums up much of what I have said and gives us a working definition:

Ecclesia is a transfigured mode of human community, an image of God's project for the world embodied in a diversity of historical churches, comprising a plurality of peoples and cultural traditions, founded upon the life, death, and resurrection of Christ, created by the redemptive presence of God as Spirit. It is a community in which privatistic, provincial, and hierarchical modes of existence are challenged and being overcome, and in which is fragmentarily actualized a universal reconciling love that liberates from sin and death, alienation and oppression.[58]

Third interlude: journey to vulnerability

The carriages were crammed with sweating humanity, mostly
soldiers. They are all young village boys dressed as soldiers,
except they carry real machine guns and look ready to use
them at the slightest provocation. The occasional presence of
a senior officer is reassuring. This ethnic conflict in Sri Lanka
has given these unemployed lads from the villages status and
meaning. Even their deaths, I am told, will bring money to
their hard-pressed families. After two weeks in this volatile
country I am sickened by the stories of violence. From mid-
night to 6.00 a.m. the train clattered on its way over the
mountains from Kandy to Bandarawella. Disturbing dreams!
I must have dozed off. It is light. We arrive soon. The mists are
clearing to reveal breathtaking scenery.

Why am I making this journey from Colombo to
Alukalavita? I came to Asia searching for something. Inspired
by Thomas Merton's Asian journey, I came with the idea of
visiting the stone carvings of the Buddha at Polonnaruwa.
Merton found enlightenment there, would I? I never got to
Polonnaruwa. When I made inquiries I was told that I only
stood a 50 per cent chance of returning alive. The risk seemed
rather high and my courage failed me; but I was to discover
what I was looking for. Instead of going north I journeyed
south. A Roman Catholic bishop, a Buddhist monk, a
Catholic theologian, the Methodist principal of a theological
college and an Anglican priest all spoke of a certain Father
Michael: 'the most creative theologian in Asia'. I had not
planned such a visit but all theological roads pointed to him.
A stay at Alukalavita became inevitable.

I have left the train and boarded the No. 29 bus. I do not feel
well and begin to regret making this trip. The bus rattles on. A
child sitting next to me has just been sick all over my foot. At
least the volume of the deafening pop music inflicted on the
passengers has been turned down. I now understand why
people become Buddhists. The ride was ceaseless torment
punctuated by scenes of indescribable beauty. We stopped at

the famous Rowana Ella Falls, where a tout managed to extract money from me, then we were back again on the bus. My ankles are swollen and smarting from mosquito bites and I feel very ill.

We are stopped by soldiers and all of us have to leave the bus and line up on the roadside. I am really scared. There is a lot of shouting and arguing. I am ignored. They pick on one man who is petrified with terror. Eventually all of us, except for this one man, are allowed back on the bus. We drive off. Looking out of the back window, I see them leading him off into the jungle. Fear and relief sweep through me.

Our driver hurls the bus around the mountain passes. Every time we grind to a halt for refreshment he tops himself up with some unmentionable brew (at one stop he had to be fetched, because he had forgotten all about us). His driving becomes maniacal as we leave the mountains behind for the arid dusty wilderness. I try to pray, but give up. The fear will not go away. I keep thinking about our fellow passenger who is with the soldiers in the jungle. What are they doing to him?

The heat is building up. At last after a nightmare journey of 22 hours we arrived at Lower Uva. Stepping from the bus was like entering an oven. The temperature, well above a hundred, strips the flesh from my bones shrivelling me up. Not far from the roadside is a collection of huts. I search around and find Sister Milberger, one of two motherly nuns who live in this tiny community.

Yes, Father Mike is here; he has fever; he has been doing too much and is exhausted; he is due to lecture in Bangladesh in a few days but will certainly not be fit enough to go. No, my letter has not arrived. He is asleep, he should not talk, he is too ill to receive visitors.

I felt confused but glad to be here, the hut was cool (well, initially) and the Sinhala charm and grace of the two nuns disarming; I wondered if I was going to see him after making this nightmare trip.

He wants to see me. As soon as I enter his room and behold this sick vulnerable man I know I am meeting a contemporary saint. Vianney Fernando, Bishop of Kandy, had spoken of how seriously people in Sri Lanka regarded St Anthony and he had drawn a parallel with Father Michael. The gentle voice and quiet eyes were enough. To see him is to love him and be loved:

> In our context it is the art of living which speaks. We Christians must leave missions behind if we are to engage in mission. Spirituality and struggle in our Buddhist context are the same. So how are we to make the move from selfishness to selflessness? We can only do this when we hear in every situation the divine imperative for the liberation of peoples. We are trying to do that here.

His words came to me like a benediction. After five minutes I had to leave. He was exhausted. I arrived weak and broken but somehow I felt I had been healed. Our conversation had immediately been about theology. We had talked as if we had met somewhere before in a distant place. He felt it too. I was held in this first meeting not by the argument nor by the penetration of his intellect but by the beauty of his language. I was too fascinated and tired to write much down. I had never before come across such integration between life, theology and speech. His theology was beautiful. It made me want to worship God.

The particular covenant invites the followers of Abraham to keep travelling in the 'far country' until their own vulnerability resonates with the pain-love of God. This, according to the covenant promise (Gen. 12.1), would become a moment of universal blessing. In this desert place of Lower Uva, and in the person of Father Michael, I had found what I was looking for.

5

From centre to edge

See how He was, hidden, teaching me to find
His face among his people.
Old hand of Sorrow, He.
Soon I was visiting them, no longer for a survey,
    bench-mark or data sheet
Or to be with them as presence, witness, what have you.
Something else (Someone) pulled me, attracted me:
His joy, his *ananda*, his peace, his *shanthi*,
Metta, karuna, mudita, upekkha; say any name's

The Name.
Somehow I found out Christ.
I went to the villages and was converted
Because He was present.
His favour called grace, made me detect
His face.[1]

Michael Rodrigo held two doctorates in theology and had
been a professor at the National Seminary, Ampitiya. Since
becoming founder-director of Subaseth Gedara he had turned
down many invitations to lecture in Europe and America. He
had also declined the offer of several professorial chairs which
might have made him an international figure. His response
was typical, 'This is where I belong, my home is with the
poor.' It is for this reason that he is not as well known in the
West as Father Aloysius Pieris, a frequent visitor to Europe.
Unlike Father Tissa Balasuriya,[2] another notable Sri Lankan
theologian who works to the background noise of his own
printing presses, Father Michael had few resources at hand.
His deteriorating eyesight had been caused by reading late
into the night under an oil lamp. He shared obscurity with the

deprived poor around him. Lack of recognition was part of his voluntary renunciation, yet nevertheless he was the most talked-about theologian in Sri Lanka.

The moral passover

In 1969 he had been granted study leave from the seminary at Ampitiya to complete his second doctorate in Paris on *Liberation in the Living Faiths of Asia: The Moral Passover from Selfishness to Selflessness in Christianity and the other Religions in Sri Lanka*.[3] On his return he found it very difficult to settle back into the seminary, which seemed unable to appreciate the radical nature of the change that had taken place in him. He said:

> It was all part of the inculturation commitment of Vatican II. Not only was theology trapped in a Western culture, I believe it has also become detached from ordinary people. The *minjung theology* of the Korean Christians offers us in Sri Lanka an appropriate model for doing theology.[4] Theology only becomes credible when it is a theology of the people, for the people, by the people.

Father Michael had come to believe that dialogue between faiths could only be intensified by making a 'moral commitment'. Dialogue deepens, he explained, when it sheds its elitism and takes into account the totality of ordinary people's lives. It intensifies further when it enters the world of passion and *dukkha* (suffering). This deeper level of dialogue cannot be achieved within an academic seminary. Rather, it must take place in a situation where people are constantly confronted with issues of life and death. In order to dialogue at depth you need to be with those who suffer most. And who are those who suffer? They are the poor. To discover the truth of the gospel we must enter their world. A moral passover is required of the theologian. Unless this takes place the theology of dialogue ceases to be liberating and becomes elitist.[5] Michael was troubled by the fact that the favoured format of interreligious dialogue was one in which the poor were systematically excluded. His experience was that entering into dialogue without the poor 'becomes only a frustrating task of aimlessly looking at each other and not transforming the world by the richness of a transforming presence'.[6]

The Wellassa area of Sri Lanka is not an ideal place to establish a Christian community. Some 160 years before, the British had left their mark:

> The people of the Uva Wellassa provinces had declared that the new regime of the Britishers was no better than the Sri Wickrema regime . . . Governor Brownrigg gave orders to Major Macdowall that all men above 18 should be killed, all houses pulled down and burnt, all trees bearing fruits of use to human beings felled, all grain either destroyed or confiscated . . . These injunctions were carried out to the letter as well. Men, women and children who would escape the sword of the British watched from the hilltops in calm and dispassionate resignation.[7]

These events are still preserved in oral tradition. Today the land is ravaged and poor; a wilderness when compared to the natural beauty of the Saccidananda Ashram. There have been climatic changes caused, in the opinion of many, by the hydro-electric scheme and the more recent destruction of the forests so that the three-month rainfall has been reduced to one month. Most of the streams have been diverted for industrial purposes, robbing the villages of water. It is a place where violence lurks beneath the surface. There are few visitors and even the theological students from the seminary are afraid to come to this hard, inhospitable place, where 99 per cent of the inhabitants are Buddhist. Father Michael came in 1980, to live with the poor. This was the first stage of 'the moral passover' enabling the dialogue with life to be intensified.[8] Like Abraham, he was called to go into the 'far country' except this was not a land where blessings multiplied; this was a land where hope died.

The dialogue with life

In 1982 the farmers in the area again lost their harvest owing to a heavy drought, so Father Michael went with some Buddhist monks to the local state official to get redress and relief. It was refused. However, the sight of Buddhists and a Christian standing together troubled the officials. That same evening the local MP contacted the leading Buddhist monk, the Venerable Alutwela Piyananda, and told him not to join with Christians in such work. The monk immediately went to see Michael and said, 'We must continue to work together . . . for whom did the Buddha work? . . . For men and women. What did your founder Christ do? He lived and died for . . . men and women.' 'So', said Michael, 'the way opened up and joint programmes were created for the killing of ignorance (*avijja*). Thus the poor became happy and the very rich unhappy because we turned our efforts towards those who in their eyes were crooks and rogues.'[9]

Father Michael was startled by what he found amongst the poor. As the poem at the head of this chapter shows, he went for theological reasons to be 'a presence, witness, what have you' and was converted. In the face of the poor he saw the face of God. Another poem, 'Buddhi and a Bottle Lamp', speaks of his discovery:

How did it begin? I don't know
I was looking into villages
And what I found burst in on me.[10]

In the apparent vulnerability of the poor he discovered the covenant God who conquers through bleeding and dying. The poor, he says, are not objects of your pity but subjects of their God-given destiny 'for with us or without us, the masses will arise'.[11] They will some day free themselves, for God uses the weak to confound the great, and equips the foolish to break the shackles of the proud. Another poem entitled 'Pieta', expressing this hope, springs from the sight of a village woman holding a father who has been crushed and killed by a tractor:

> There in your lap, we see the human face of God, the Son
> Your child.
> Back in a region, to the urban 'wild'
> Back in a region with its people, mild
> Water fountain rich in harvest
> Phoenix-like they'll rise from the ashes.[12]

The great commission: teaching

The imperative of 'make disciples' in the 'great commission' is interpreted by two participles, 'teaching' and 'baptizing'.

In the Old Testament, we have seen that Abraham is held up as the supreme example of faith. His faith is reckoned as righteousness (Gen. 15.6); his faith demonstrates itself in deeds (Jas. 2.18–24); his faith looks to the future in hope (Heb. 11.11–12). These ingredients are encapsulated in the words 'to observe all that I have commanded you' (Matt. 28. 20).

'Teaching' (*didaskontes*) is not to be understood as an intellectual enterprise which attempts to impart knowledge and insight.[13] Such a world-view is a feature of Western elitism where teachers function as depositors, prescribers and domesticators. They operate with what Paulo Freire calls the 'banking concept'.[14] Within this system the 'educated' are deemed to be those who have successfully jumped through certain academic hoops and thereby acquired personal status and power. In a devastating critique of Western academic theology, Alister McGrath argues that the theology of the academic community and that of the community of faith have become two disconnected worlds. Academic theology has marginalized itself. Not only does it cease to have relevance for the growing churches of Africa and Asia, but it has little meaning for most of the people in the churches of Britain. Academic theologians talk among themselves in an 'inflation of discourse' which comes across as 'mumbo jumbo' to people in the pew. McGrath regards the publication in 1977 of the book entitled *The Myth of God Incarnate* not only as the final disjunction between academic theologians and Christians in general but also as a notable 'own goal'.[15]

Matthew uses the word *terein* ('observe', 'keep' or 'practice') to refer to a catechetical process aimed not so much at imparting 'knowledge of the word' but of enabling people to 'do the word'. As Jesus points out:

> Every one then who hears these words of mine and does them will be like a wise man who built his house upon the rock. (Matt. 7.24)

A Jewish disciple of the *Torah* followed a rabbi until he himself became a rabbi with his own disciples. Not so the disciples of Jesus. They do not choose him, he chooses them. Moreover they never graduate into rabbis, though they can become apostles. In other words, the disciples of Jesus 'disciple as part of their own discipleship'. This immediately blurs the distinction between teacher and learner because in the kingdom of heaven 'a disciple is not above his teacher, nor a servant above his master' (Matt. 10.24). Father Michael, because of his understanding of Buddhism, knew that the word must always be the 'active word'. He also found that, in going to teach the poor, the poor became his teacher:

> The Old Testament held Christ in its loins and the New Testament brought Him forth as the Word made flesh. The God of the Bible did not reveal Jesus to us. It was Jesus who revealed God to us . . . Christ is the Word but he is principally the 'doing Word'. He is the active verb of God. He leaves his footprints across the wastes of the world and it is for us to tread in them . . . Buddhism stresses the importance of living out one's enlightenment, for wisdom (*panna*) is knowledge which makes us act correctly.[16]

Michael held that the violent context of Sri Lanka demanded

a theological agenda which examined the discrepancies between theory and practice. A theology of dialogue is not about a mode of thinking but about a way of acting. The *logos* is found inside 'dia-logue' thus the transforming presence of the Word within the world is the starting point for all meeting. Through dialogue we are able to discern God's face (*panim*) just as Jacob did when he met with Esau (Gen. 33.10).[17]

The great commission: baptizing

Physical circumcision is the authentic mark of being within the covenant established with Abraham. Baptism, depicting a circumcision of the heart, is the physical sign of becoming a member of the new ecclesial community (Col. 2.11–12). Tissa Balasuriya begins his book *Planetary Theology* with these words:

> It puzzles and saddens me that so many who call themselves Christian are so little concerned about the immense human misery and suffering in almost all parts of the world. Sometimes we are even the cause of this suffering and we seem not to realize it. Our going regularly to Church and attending prayer services seem to leave us uninterested in the fate of our sisters and brothers. On the contrary, our being considered good Christians may be what makes us insensitive to them.[18]

Just as we have to rethink our notion of teaching, so our interpretation of 'baptizing' (*baptizontes*), requires radical revision. Jesus, in submitting to John's baptism of repentance, freely and willingly establishes a gracious solidarity with us as sinners so fulfilling 'all righteousness' (Matt. 3.15). 'When Jesus had himself baptized with water by John, he began the fulfilment of his mission as the Son of the Father who had come into the world to reconcile it to God.'[19] At a stroke the event of the Jordan and the event of Golgotha are joined to the event of Pentecost:[20]

I came to cast fire upon the earth; and would that it were already kindled! I have a baptism to be baptized with; and how I am constrained until it is accomplished (Lk. 12.49–50).

Dr V. C. Samuel from Bangalore says, 'baptism proclaims that God is creating a new world and a new man of the old world'.[21] Under the rainbow, baptism becomes the sign of liberation into a new humanity [22] where the divisions of race, sex and social class are transcended. We can therefore no longer think of baptism as an individualistic rite of washing, a sacramental displacement activity incorporating us into a warm, snug community. Baptism is not a return trip into the still safe waters of the womb, instead it calls us along with Abraham, Moses and Father Michael, to undertake an outward-bound journey into the wildernesses of the world (Mk 1.12).[23] Aloysius Pieris invites the Church to undergo a new baptism. He says that our Lord's action in fulfilling all righteousness through baptism was a prophetic act of asceticism and identification with the 'religious poor'. A church so baptized becomes a learning church rather than a teaching church:[24]

> It is unjustifiable to regard the 'great commission' as being concerned primarily with 'evangelism' and the 'great commandment' (Matt. 22.37–40) as referring to 'social involvement'. As Jacques Matthey puts it; according to Matthew's 'great commission', it is not possible to make disciples without telling them to practise God's call of justice for the poor. The love commandment, which is the basis for the Church's involvement in politics, is an integral part of the mission commandment.[25]

Teaching and baptizing in the name of the Father, the Son and the Holy Spirit is therefore God's way of calling us from the centre to the edge. It invites us to establish solidarity with the poor, the marginalized and the excluded.

Baptism calls us to a life of self-emptying or *kenosis*, leading to the death (*nekrosis*) of our very selves.[26] Baptism under the rainbow has more to do with spilling blood than sprinkling water. Incarnation, kingdom and discipleship are integral to Matthew's understanding of mission.[27] Teaching and baptizing, as interpreted above, are invitations to the 'imitation of Christ'. The evangelical poverty, so obvious in the 'moral passover' of Father Michael, is a poverty which belongs to the beatitudes.[28] As we saw in Chapter 3, the great commission commands Christians to undertake a journey into a 'far country', in the expectation of meeting the great I AM. The 'great commission', as we are beginning to see in this chapter, calls us to imitate the Christ who, in his own incarnation, replicated the vulnerability and triumph of the God of grace who journeys through time and space.

Milestones to exclusion and crusade

Father Bede and Father Michael bring a sharp critique to the Western missionary enterprise, which they regard as having been shaped by exclusive and triumphalist theologies. We have attempted to win the whole world for Christ by inappropriate means and have rightly failed. Wearing theological blinkers, we pursue the wrong goals using the wrong methods. Where did these blinkers come from? Why are we trapped within this exclusive crusading framework? This perspective, I want to argue, has been formed by the contingencies of our own history. I can best explain by describing briefly some important milestones on the road to exclusivism and triumphalism.

The first milestone was the prohibitive contract between Church and state. Christians of the first century managed to live with a plurality of theologies, liturgies and patterns of ministry. We see something of this diversity within the New Testament itself.[29] For the first few hundred years general agreement about a rule of faith and acceptance of the New Testament canon was deemed sufficient. Local unity and theological integrity was focused in the person of the bishop. However, important changes took place in the fourth century as the Church began to assume a more dominating role within the Roman Empire and as the Empire itself, 'like a fortress surrounded by turbulent seas', was threatened by wave upon wave of barbarian invasions.[30] This collusion between Church and state had the effect of limiting plurality of ecclesial expression. It also served to outlaw certain forms of church life. Some inculturated models of Christianity, like that of the Donatists in North Africa, were prohibited by the use of state force. The influential bishops of Rome and Alexandria, who were now becoming political figures, spoke of there being no salvation outside the Church. They meant their church. Exclusive institutional boundaries were being defined.

The second milestone was the division of Christendom. The accommodation between God and Caesar, described above, began with Constantine who in AD 312 became both a Christian and a victorious Roman emperor. Along with the new state religion of Christianity, he provided the Empire with a new capital city at the neck of the Bosporus, named Constantinople.[31] In the harsh century which followed, the Western civilization of Rome was ravaged and vandalized while the Eastern remnant of what had been the Roman Empire continued in the old way.[32] With this severing of connections between Eastern and Western Christianity the cosmic dimension of salvation found in Eastern thinkers like Clement, Origen and the Cappadocian Fathers was lost to the West.[33] The more inclusive 'logos' theology faded before a dominant Western Augustinianism. The emerging Church in the West became increasingly suspicious of any variant to its one institutionalized presentation of Christianity. Variants were regarded as deviant. There was now only 'one ecclesiastical way' to the Father.

The third milestone was the crusading response of Christians, in the eleventh century, to Islam.[34] Islam arose partly because of the failure of Christianity to bring cohesion to the various warring Arabic factions and partly as a prophetic protest against a religion which, in their eyes, had reverted to paganism through its doctrine of the Trinity. Christians, like Jews, were no longer regarded as the true spiritual heirs of Abraham.[35] The Church, threatened by the rapid advance of this new desert religion, reacted aggressively. For the next few hundred years soldiers of Christ put their armour on, often over their priestly robes, and rode out to do battle.[36] Evangelism became a holy war; a fight to the death against the enemies of Christ. Crusade is a most powerful expression of Christian idealism. The ecclesiastical leaders of these missions were no longer called abbots, fathers and mothers but generals. Infidels without and heretics within had to be vanquished; thus a massacre of Jews in Germany launched every crusade.[37] Caged in for nearly five hundred years by Islam on the Eastern and Southern boundaries, it is hardly surprising that many Christians, unable to appreciate that God might be speaking outside the Church, were antagonistic to other faiths. With the opening up of the New World, fresh opportunities for crusade were offered. Having failed to win the battle against Islam in Europe, the Church went out to conquer 'other worlds' for Christ.[38] Latin America still bears the scars of this violent campaign. The native North American Indians say 'when the Europeans came, we had land and they had the Bible, but now we have the Bible and they have the land'.[39] This third milestone is probably the most significant of all, for deeply rooted in the Western ecclesial subconscious is the slogan 'mission is crusade'.

Islam, together with Christianity and Judaism, has significantly shaped European culture. This culture, since the Enlightenment, has become increasingly pagan and secular much to the dismay of Muslims. The resurgence of militant forms of Islam since the 1970 oil crisis must be seen as a dramatic protest against creeping secularism and technological imperialism.[40]

Away from crusade?

John V. Taylor gives us two contrasting Franciscan stories. The first concerns St Francis's strange meeting with Sala'din. They had no common language, so little dialogue can have taken place. Yet near the end of the encounter Sala'din is reported to have said, 'If ever I meet a second Christian like you I would be willing to be baptized. But that will not happen.' Three hundred years later there was a horribly different sort of encounter between a Franciscan friar, who accompanied the Conquistadores, and the king of the vanquished Incas of Peru. The friar offered him a choice: conversion or death. The king hesitated and his hands were cut off. The appeal was repeated, 'Be baptized and you will go to heaven.' 'No,' said the king, 'for if I went to heaven I might meet a second Christian like you!'[41]

Our Western theological and cultural mindset has conditioned us to single out an exclusive text like John 14.6, 'no one comes to the Father but by me', and made us blind to those more inclusive passages of Scripture described in Chapter 2. This mindset, formed and hardened in our unconscious by nearly fifteen hundred years of crusading zeal, is not going to shift easily.

Father Michael's 'moral passover' is a journey from the centre to the edge. It requires the shedding of elitism, the casting off of 'powers' and a radical letting go. We face, it has been suggested,[42] a situation comparable to that of the Council of Jerusalem in AD 49 when the leaders of the mother Church decided to drop most of the Jewish cultic requirements so that non-Jews could become God's people without becoming Jews. Of course only a few like Paul, who struggled to forge a new inclusive theology, recognized the far-reaching implications of that decision. A similar shift is required of us to allow non-Western Christians to become Christians in their way and not ours. It also raises radical questions about the nature and purpose of Christianity as we have traditionally understood it. The Latin-American theologian José

Miguez Bonino, in words which burn with passion, puts the challenge:

> I sense that there is a tendency to think that evangelism can remain unaffected, can carry on business as usual, without forgetting social action, but without being fundamentally changed. This, it seems to me, is to be a deadly misunderstanding. The real problem is that the alliance of missions and Western capitalistic expansion has distorted the Gospel beyond recognition, and that evangelism, prayer, worship and personal devotions have been held captive to an individualistic, otherworldly, success-crazy, legalistic destruction of the Gospel. Evangelism, prayer, worship and private devotions do not have to be abandoned. They have to be converted to Christ.[43]

A world of violence

Peter, who had preached 'there is no other name' (Acts 4.12), is forced in his encounter with Cornelius (Acts 10) to enter the topsy-turvy world of God's extra-mural activities. He confesses, 'I now realize how true it is that God does not show favouritism but accepts men from every nation who fear him and do what is right' (Acts 10.34).

Unfortunately such open-heartedness is in short supply. In today's violent world, tribalism and triumphalism is on the increase. The bloody ethnic conflict in what was former Yugoslavia was a symptom of a growing listlessness in Europe from which terrorist and neo-Fascist groups profit. The attack on the Pentagon and World Trade Center in Manhattan was a revelatory event, waking us from our complacent slumbers to the dangers posed by the religious fanatic and the terrorist. The bitter cycle of violence between Israel and the Palestinians; the 'war against terrorism'; the military assault on Iraq; and the fear of chemical attacks in London, all are warning indicators of a growing global insecurity. As with Noah's flood, the primal waters of chaos are starting to engulf us, but they come not from outside the so-called 'civilized world' but from the sizzling cracks that are opening up in our midst. These destructive outpourings can be seen as a negative by-product of the Western civilizing enterprise.[44] We are reaping the consequences of our insularity and lack of enthusiasm in pursuing social and economic justice for all the nations of the earth.

Philip Jenkins, in his chilling book *The Next Christendom*, suggests that the very expansion of Christianity and Islam across countries and within countries may provoke future civil wars and fuel fanatical religious conflicts. He holds that the day of the crusade is not over. Indeed we stand on the threshold of 'the next crusade'.[45] He presents us with a bleak future as Muslims and Christians blunder into new conflicts, and he asks us to imagine what it would be like to live in the world of the thirteenth century where solders instead of carrying swords and shields are armed with nuclear warheads and anthrax.[46]

The writings of René Girard expose the root of violence and track 'the little streams that flow into the great rivers of collective violence'.[47] The violence which provoked God (Gen. 6.6) and triggered the holocaust of the flood had its beginning in Cain. Cain was not only the first murderer, he was also the founder of a culture.[48] This thread of murder and violence runs through the story of humanity, for violence is mimetic; it imitates itself.[49] We saw it in the crusades and it keeps revealing itself in different guises. This mimetic contagion spawns bigotry, victims and scapegoats. Girard argues that in a culture, where scapegoats are no longer concealed by religion, those who use them genuinely believe they are not doing so.[50] The relationship between 9/11 and the war in Iraq in 2003 is therefore far more subtle than the polemics of war would have us believe.

Western theology, influenced by centuries of crusade, was largely designed to protect the limits of what we have come to regard as Christian. Ecclesiastical politicians, ministers and priests preside like theological policemen at the boundaries, setting up signs and markers to protect the chosen people who dwell in the inner sanctuary.[51] It is assumed that people from the 'far country' should see things as we do. Donald Messer argues that we are called to become a community of fence 'movers'. The fences are to be 'moved' not 'removed'.[52] Fences are necessary to exclude 'the arrow that flies by day and the pestilence that stalks the darkness' (Ps. 91.5). They must be extended to include all people of goodwill (which in our terms means all who pursue the universal mandates of the rainbow covenant). But here again even a tiny movement will be difficult because many fences are maintained by toxic ideologies and sustained by mimetic violence.

The response of many Christians in the rich nations will, I suspect, be reactionary and violent. Notions of a 'jealous God' have been a powerful incentive for crusade and arise from the 'shadow side' of our existence, that sump within which the rejected parts of ourselves are dumped.[53] Here dwells 'mimetic desire': the jealous root which spawns self-distrust, fear of aliens, anger, pride, ambition, unresolved sexuality and all those monsters which fuel violence. Given certain economic and sociological conditions, these powerful feelings can erupt and be scapegoated onto groups and individuals who appear different from ourselves.[54] The paranoid wars of religion, persecution of the Jews and other minorities, racism, sexism, the demonizing of Islam, the different fundamentalisms and inordinate acts of retribution draw demonic strength from this abyss. Breaking the mimetic cycle and the abandonment of crusades and scapegoats will demand nothing less than a dying and a rebirth of our understanding of ourselves both as human beings and as Christians. The conversion is required of us has to be more lasting than Peter's (Gal. 2.11–13). If we do not eat what at first sight seems theologically distasteful (Acts 10.14), we may, like Jonah, be consumed by our own bigotry:

And Jonah stalked
to his shaded seat
and waited for God

78

to come around
to his way of thinking.
And God is still waiting for a host of Jonahs
in their comfortable houses
to come around
to his way of loving.[55]

A counter-cultural ecclesial community

The Subaseth Gedera community, planted by Father Michael, is a sign of grace and gratitude in a wilderness of despair and in a country of violence. Here the particularity of the pain-love of God is given authentic expression. Abraham's descendants were called to leave God's 'footprints' across history. This ecclesial community, since its particularity enables the universality of God's grace to be recognized, is one of those 'counter-cultural' footprints. Father Michael insisted, much to the bewilderment of the Buddhists, that the educational programme be opened to everyone, especially to the less favoured, because education is for justice and improving the lot of all.[56] The teaching was designed to help people 'live the Word' which is both the *Torah* of Jesus and the *Dharma* of Buddha.

The local Buddhist monk, after studying with Michael, encouraged his people to come, saying, 'he has responded in his heart and is to us a Buddhist'. The best testimony comes from a young Buddhist man who said:

Because the Church truly lays claim to too much wealth and property, she cannot change the existing unjust system. There are 99 per cent Buddhists in this area and for about five years this little group has honoured our traditional and time-honoured customs and culture . . . we watched you at the start . . . did you come to turn us to your ways somehow? . . . I now see after these years that this little Christian group has understood our sorrows, our plight and are very loving and compassionate towards the poor . . . All this proves the true meaning of your house, Subaseth Gedara . . . Good wishes house.[57]

There was strong episcopal pressure on the community to baptize, but Father Michael resisted. Baptism had already taken place through the identification of the Christian community with the poor and lost. Like baptism, the 'moral passover' is both voluntary and permanent. There can be no going back. 'You do not live with the poor for a time and then withdraw, for you are choosing truth, beauty and joy.' Then he paused; and after a long silence quoted words which will forever be engraved on my heart:

I thought that my voyage had come to its end at the last limit of my power; that the path before me was closed; that provisions were exhausted and the time come to take shelter in silent obscurity. But I find that Thy will, O God, knows no end in me. And when old words die out on the tongue, new melodies break forth from the heart; and where the old tracks are lost, a new country is revealed with all its wonders.[58]

So in the 'far country' my last conversation with Father Michael ended. We sat in silence sharing the deep peace which had intensified between us. I asked if I could take a photo of him. With a sparkle of fun he said, 'Well, I had better put my teeth in.' And he did.

Back to Abraham

We started with Abraham and we end with him. His journey began, says Miroslav Volf, when he became aware of the Babel abyss of non-being around him.[59] His departure can be seen both as an act of judgement on the culture in which he had settled and also as an act of judgement on himself as part of that culture. The irony was that his descendants were to become ensnared by settlement and so lose their ability to be radically self-critical. God is persistent in his intention of breaking the cycle of mimetic violence. His message to Abraham, his Jewish children's children and to the new ecclesial community is that God is creating a new world in which:

> people from every nation and every tribe, with their cultural goods, will gather around the triune God, a world in which every tear will be wiped away and pain will be no more (Rev. 21.3). Christians distance themselves from their own culture because they give the ultimate allegiance to God and to God's promised future.[60]

This 'passing over' avoids the traps of mimetic violence and sets up the conditions for the creation of a 'new space' into which others can enter and become covenant partners with God. To obey Abraham's and our Lord's mandate to 'go' (Gen. 12.1; Matt. 28.18) is to be born of the Spirit who seeks to send us from the familiar so as to create a new future for us, for the world and for God.

6

A covenant in the Spirit

'But you shall receive power when the Holy Spirit has come upon you; and you shall be my witnesses in Jerusalem and in all Judea and Samaria and to the end of the earth.' (Acts 1.8)

Grace and election are the first two theological ingredients of covenant, the third is 'spirit'. The prophet Jeremiah looks to the day when God will forge a new covenant and write the divine mandates on the hearts of people (Jer. 31.31–4). The Old Testament ends with the vision of all Israel sharing in God's Spirit (Ezek. 36.27), of the Spirit being carried on 'wagons of wind' to the four corners of the earth (Zech. 6.1–8)[1] and poured out on all flesh (Joel 2.28).

The Hebrew word *ruach*, can be translated 'breath', 'wind' or 'spirit'.[2] The Spirit was active in creating the cosmos, brooding over the formless chaos (Gen. 1.2). This 'toxic void' of chaos was a primal mess in which everything was jumbled up. God begins by 'separating' light from darkness, day from night, water from land. At the same time he 'binds' things together: humans to the rest of creation, himself to us as bearers of his image.[3] This activity of 'separation-and-binding' is covenantal, reflecting the Trinity in whom persons are both distinct and together. Creation happens through the 'word of the Lord' and by the 'breath (Spirit) of his mouth' (Ps. 33.6). Just as through his 'Word' the triune God is active 'toward' creation, so in his 'Spirit' he is active 'in' creation. John Taylor, one-time General Secretary of the Church Missionary Society, in his book *The Go-Between God*, says that the Word gives order and direction while the Spirit gives energy and inspiration.[4]

Nevertheless there is something primal and wild about

ruach.[5] The Spirit who broods over creation also sweeps across Noah's flood, drying up the waters. The Spirit like a gale drives back the waters of the Red Sea.[6] This same Spirit is the hurricane wind which sweeps across the desert demolishing the house of Job (Job 1.19) and later revealing the majesty of God (Job 38.1). The Spirit is the storm wind that passes judgement on Jonah's ship preventing him from fleeing to Tarshish (Jon. 1.4); it is the scorching wind that burns up his shade and blows away his tiny conception of God (Jon. 4.8). It is the great wind which rattles the bones in Ezekiel's death valley, puts flesh on them and resurrects an army (Ezek. 37.1–14). This Spirit is God's instrument of life and death:

> When you take away their breath (*ruach*), they die and return to the dust.
> When you send your Spirit (*ruach*), they are created; and you renew the face of the earth. (Ps. 104.29–30)

Life-giving energies of such consequence are released by this primal Spirit that safety is abandoned. Does the Spirit then represent the wild, untamed dimension in God? Has the Spirit been let out, as it were, to play like a child? Certainly playing and the release of the child within is essential for creativity, but the Spirit is not detached from God. The person of the Holy Spirit, along with the Father and Son, also shares in the risk and pain of this creative adventure of partnership. Like the nervous system in the human body, the Holy Spirit sensing the slightest imbalance in the cosmos articulates the pain in 'groans which words cannot express' (Rom. 8.22, 26). The Spirit, at the same time, seeks to ameliorate and heal the distress by attempting to restore 'connectedness' within creation. He both startles his creatures and inspires in them the necessity of choice. Thus freedom is given by the Spirit through the elective processes of the Word.

The Holy Spirit is the midwife, the mother and the child of creation. These activities are often associated with female qualities but it would be inappropriate to identify the Spirit as the 'token female within the God-head'[7] for vulnerability lies at the heart of the triune, covenant God of grace. The empowering Spirit, however, specializes in creative irrationality. She cannot be tamed and the Church cannot domesticate her. She indwells the whole created order and is the contact person of mission. Taylor says, 'The chief actor in the historic mission of the Christian Church is the Holy Spirit. He is the director of the whole enterprise.'[8]

A *new covenant of brokenness and blessing*

Each of the enigmatic covenant signs contain elements of hope and suffering. The rainbow of promise is also the 'war bow' of pain. The strange Abrahamic ceremony of blood and sacrifice (Gen. 15. 9–21) mingles inheritance and hope with the obligation of circumcision and obedience. The new covenant is a new exodus Passover of broken bread and poured out wine; symbolic ingredients of sacrifice and thanksgiving; a portrayal of grace and gratitude. 'This is my body' (Matt. 26.26; Mk 14.22; Lk. 22.19; 1 Cor. 11.24). 'This is my blood of the new covenant' (Matt. 26.28; Mk 14.24; Lk. 22.20; 1 Cor. 11.25).[9] While this is a covenant of brokenness, it is also a covenant of blessing.

The former covenants signal a 'going forth', a sending, a mission. This new covenant is no exception. The last words of the old Latin mass were: *ite missa est*; 'Go out now, you are being sent.' In the Last Supper Jesus uses the parabolic method of the great prophets of old (Jer. 27.2) to drive home the unpalatable truth that he must be broken like the bread and poured out like wine. The embracing pain-love of God here receives its supreme expression.

From the birth of the universe we hear echoes of God's suffering. His gracious covenant with Noah follows an episode of shame when the whole world is drowned in an ocean of God's tears.[10] In the stories which follow, the hidden God tramps through history faithfully holding fast to the covenant, which we keep breaking, always making space for humanity within himself.[11] We behold a Trinitarian God so identified with Israel that God in Christ lives out in himself the tragic history of this chosen people. The truth about God's self-giving goes even further. Such is his solidarity with Abraham's people that Jesus Christ, in both exposing Israel's sin and God's condemnation of it, lives out the experience of being under the judgement of God (Isa. 53.8f.). In this new covenant Jesus Christ is broken. Through his brokenness and death the 'pain' of God is revealed, for this God 'is not greater than he is in this humiliation. God is not more glorious than he is in this helplessness. God is not more divine than he is in this humanity.'[12]

Within the covenant, not only are we accountable to God for our sin but also God makes himself accountable to us. Moreover for love's sake, he has chosen to hold himself responsible for the tragedies of creation. This is now fully revealed in this new covenant of brokenness for there can be no gospel unless God is shown to have integrity.[13] The apostle Paul, in his exposition of 'justification' in Romans 3.25–6, argues that the righteousness of God has to be set out in two senses: 'to prove [i.e. show] at this present time that he [God] himself is righteous and [second] that he justifies him who has faith in Jesus' (v. 26). Sin's consequences are so disastrous that a simple act of forgiveness would compromise God's righteousness. Thus if the holy God is to forgive, he must at the same time do it in such a way as to show that he is still a righteous God.[14] 'Paul recognizes that what is at stake is not just God's being "seen" to be righteous, but of God "being" righteous.'[15]

In the death of Christ the internalized 'wrath of God' is given external expression, as the pain of God is shown to be 'real' pain.[16] In this focused cathartic activity the wounds of God are cauterized and cleansed. In the breaking and pouring out of Jesus we are given a sign more glorious than the rainbow and a symbol which cuts more deeply than circumcision. On Golgotha's hill, the Eternal Heart of Love misses a beat and the universe convulses in agony. All relationships within the cosmos are changed.[17] All creation can now be told that the God who accepts responsibility for the tragic existence of evil is a God to be trusted for he, out of his love for us, has judged himself and embraced the pain of all things.

According to Claus Westermann, there are two methods used by God for the good of humankind: the way of deliverance and the way of blessing.[18] The word 'bless' (*barak*) means to 'give power, vigour and strength'. Abraham's entire vocation is motivated by the promise of blessing. The Hebrew word for covenant (*berith*) is directly related to the words 'create' and 'bless'. Blessing is not an abstraction; it is about enjoying and sharing life's basic gifts. The promised land was to provide Abraham's children with a space in which to celebrate the fertility of the God who embraces the stranger, heals the earth and regenerates the ecosystem. God's final objective is nothing less than the overcoming of mimetic violence and the recreation of a new living space for everyone and everything. This is possible because he has made a space for us within the dancing life of the Trinity. 'When the Trinity turns towards the world, the Son and the Spirit become, in Irenaeus's beautiful image, the two arms of God by which humanity was made and taken into God's embrace.'[19] So the Eucharistic blessing in the Last Supper is Trinitarian, universal, cosmic, spiritual, physical and eschatological. It anticipates the great feast at the end of time when rainbow blessings abound. Then all the dark shadows of violence, disease and death will be removed for ever (Isa. 25.6f.). It will be a time of dance (Ex. 15.20), laughter (Ps. 126.2) and loving (Song 5.1), for the end is the transfiguration of all things. God's blessing:

> brings joy to every creature. It clothes the naked tree; it opens the earth. It produces joy in all the animals . . . this is for Christians . . . the time of resurrection in which their bodies will be glorified by means of the light which even now is in them hiddenly; this is the power of the Spirit who will then be their clothing, food, drink, exultation, gladness, peace, adornment, and eternal life.[20]

The new covenant mandates

The Last Supper is a culmination of a whole series of meals, table fellowships (Matt. 8.11; Lk. 13.29; 17.27; 22.30), weddings (Matt. 22.2f.; Jn 2.1f.), eating and drinking (Mk 2.16), 'music and dancing' (Lk. 15.25). This sacramental meal should be interpreted from an understanding of all the other gospel meals.[21] It must also have a future orientation.[22] Embedded in this meal are four liturgical actions which, according to Gregory Dix,[23] are the invariable nucleus of every eucharistic rite throughout antiquity.

Offering	(Jesus took bread)
Thanksgiving or blessing	(Jesus gave thanks)
Fraction	(Jesus broke the bread)
Sharing	(Jesus gave)

These actions are held together by the dominical command, 'Do this in remembrance of me.' In the taking, blessing, breaking and giving of bread the real presence of Christ is recalled; indeed in one post-resurrection meal the risen Christ is visibly revealed in the breaking of bread (Lk. 24.30). Because of the presence of the Holy Spirit, the first Christians believed they were eating and drinking 'with' the risen Christ.[24]

But there is a further surprise! These four actions occur in all accounts of the feeding of the five thousand (and the four thousand) (Matt. 14.19; 15.36; Mk 6.41; 8.6; Lk. 9.16; Jn 6.11). The authenticity of this miracle cannot be easily dismissed, recorded as it is in all four Gospels. Commentators struggle to make sense of it. I see it as the climax of the first phase of our Lord's early ministry, a sort of 'dress rehearsal for the Messianic feast'.[25]

Vincent Taylor writing of this feeding miracle says, 'Mark has conformed the vocabulary of the passage to that of the Last Supper in the belief that in some sense the fellowship meal in the wilderness was an anticipation of the Eucharist.'[26] Others make little of the connection.[27] Let us look at it through a missiological lens rather than through a liturgical one. Could it be that Jesus at the Last Supper is reminding the disciples of this miracle of feeding in the wilderness? They did not understand it the first time round (Mk 6.52; 8.17–19). Could it be that Jesus is in effect saying:

> Remember what I did on that occasion! You failed to meet the needs of people then. You did not understand what I did or how I did it! I want you to try again. You must keep re-enacting this feeding in the wilderness so that I can come and celebrate the end-time messianic feast with all humanity.

Such an exposition is not generally pursued since most scholars quite naturally interpret the actions from a 'liturgical' rather than a 'missiological' point of view. It could be argued that such actions at the meal table were, in any case, common-place and have no special significance. If we do link the feeding miracle with the Eucharist in the way I have suggested, then the implication is very disturbing. Tissa Balasuriya in his *Eucharist and Liberation* takes this line and asks, 'Why hasn't the Eucharist worked?'

> For two thousand years the churches have continued to celebrate the Eucharist in his memory . . . Millions of men, women and children have drawn personal inspiration through the centuries from the Eucharist. . . On the other hand, Christians have divided themselves into different sects partly on their views concerning the Eucharist . . . But even more tragic is the way the Eucharist has been domesticated within the dominant social establishment of the day. Its radical demands have been largely neutralized . . . Worse still, it has been used and is being used as a legitimization of cruel exploitation . . . Why is it that in spite of hundreds and thousands of Eucharistic celebrations, Christians continue as selfish as before? . . . Why is the gap of income, wealth, knowledge, and power growing in the world today?[28]

By splitting it off from the feeding of the five thousand, we have spiritualized the Last Supper and at one stroke removed the corporate, social, political and ecological dimensions. We have tamed the ferocity of the Eucharist by placing it in a comfortable ecclesiastical setting rather than in the desert wastes of the world. We have McDonaldized it, turning the Eucharist into an ecclesiastical fast food.[29] Once the Eucharist was linked with the sharing of goods. That is no longer the case. Once it was set in the context of a corporate meal. Now it has been privatized. 'Negatively the Eucharist is a protest, a critique. It protests against unequal structures in society. It protests against the abuse of material. It protests against injustice and inhumanity. Its function then is to disturb . . . '[30] The miracle we should seek to comprehend is not how wine can be turned into blood but how people living in the wildernesses of the world can be given a taste of the new wine of the Spirit.

Luke's theological presentation of the baptism of the Holy Spirit (Acts 2.5–11) reverses the destructive effects of Babel. Universal communication and the prophetic dream of a new 'rainbow community', made up of peoples from every nation on earth, are realized:

All the believers were together and had everything in common. Selling their possessions and goods, they gave to anyone as he had need. Every day they continued to meet together in the temple courts. They broke bread in their homes and ate together with glad and sincere hearts, praising God and enjoying the favour of all the people. And the Lord added to their number daily those who were being saved. (Acts 2.44–7)

An ecclesial community has been formed by the Holy Spirit. The Eucharist is 'for those who have an intimate sharing fellowship which prompts them to share material wealth with those with whom they communicate'.[31] It is a community which does not exclude but embraces humankind. It is a community where the root of mimetic violence has been removed.

It is a community where people, through sharing, prayer and praise, demonstrate grace and gratitude. Ecclesial communities have a liturgical and a missionary calling.[32] Girard asks, 'What is this power that triumphs over mimetic violence?' He answers, 'The Gospels respond that it is the Spirit of God, the third person of the Trinity, the Holy Spirit.'[33]

A liturgical and missionary vocation

The miracle of Pentecost happens in the context of prayer and praise. Prayer is not something we do for the benefit of our own spiritual health. It is one of the instruments of mission. Because we are partners with God in mission, prayer not only opens us up to God, prayer enables God to accomplish the things he chooses not to do without us. In praying, we ourselves run the risk of becoming one of God's obedient instruments for bringing about what we pray for. When we intercede on matters of injustice, or bring to God the pain of victims of violence, we are offering him an opening into the world so that he is able to work good in situations of anguish.[34] Through prayer we help to make the world a little more 'porous to divine reality'.[35]

But there is even more to prayer than this, for God himself is 'moved' because of our prayers. Bible prayers are punctuated with protest, lament and praise. Abraham, looking towards Sodom, raises questions about God's arithmetic. God listens to his protest and reviews his own actions (Gen. 18.16–33).[36] Jeremiah complains about God's indecision (Jer. 20.7–12). God has to decide what sort of God he is going to be.[37] Through the hymns of Paul and Silas (Acts 16.25–6) prison doors are blown open. Because of the praise of the apostolic church God renews the Pentecostal experience and pours out fresh gifts on the apostles (Acts 4.24–31). Prayer and praise in the Holy Spirit become the means whereby 'boldness' and 'mighty deeds' (*dunameis*) are bestowed as power tools for mission.

In the first century, state religion had become so bankrupt

and tired[38] that boldness and enthusiasm were regarded as little short of madness. The boldness of the apostles agitated the authorities (Acts 5.27–33). Paul's passionate preaching upset the cultured Athenians (Acts 17.16–32). The Roman Governor Festus was disturbed by the enthusiasm of Paul's testimony (Acts 26.24). At the beginning of the second century, in official correspondence between the emperor Trajan and one of his civil servants Pliny, we read that Christians continue to be 'afflicted with like madness' and are therefore punished for 'their stubbornness and unyielding obstinacy'.[39] A passionate advocacy of faith is one of the by-products of baptism by the Holy Spirit.

The Holy Spirit also gave the apostles the ability to work miracles (Mk 16.17–18). The book of Acts abounds in mighty deeds: the gift of languages on the day of Pentecost, a crippled beggar walks (3.1–12), the exorcisms (8.6–7), Paul's healing of the lame man at Lystra (14.8–11) and spectacular events in Ephesus (19.11–20). In many cases these miracles create a platform from which the apostles speak a word of interpretation. However, it is their lifestyle rather than their boldness and miracle working which becomes the enduring cutting-edge of mission. From the sharing of bread and wine in the Eucharist flows the desire to share all material resources (Acts 2.44; 4.32–5). This deeply challenged the values of the Roman world. 'Christians', according to one early commentator, 'shared their goods, their meals, their worship, everything except their wives', which was often the only thing pagans were willing to share. The emperor Julian was equally provoked by the lifestyle of Christians:

> Atheism [the name for Christianity] has been specially advanced through the loving service rendered to strangers, and through their care for the burial of the dead. It is a scandal that there is not a single Jew who is a beggar, and that the godless Galileans [Christians] care not only for their own poor but for ours as well.[40]

This demonstration of community (*koinonia*) through the Spirit was essentially holistic, economic and practical.[41] Luke sees it as an enactment of the Old Testament dream of Jubilee (Lev. 25) when the oppressed were set free and resources restored (Lk. 4.18–19; 19.1–10). For Paul, the word *koinonia* was often a synonym for 'collection'. Tirelessly visiting the Gentile churches, he attempted to raise money for the poor in Jerusalem so giving a practical demonstration of the *koinonia* of the body of Christ.[42] 'What God does in the world as Spirit, is to engender spiritual community.'[43] The New Testament apostolic Church incarnates something of God's dream of a rainbow, counter-cultural community.

When liturgy catches fire, disciples become apostles and receive the same anointing as Jesus at his baptism.[44] This baptism of the Spirit not only initiates mission but also enables the missionaries to be guided by the Spirit who tells them where to go and what to do. The wind of the Spirit scatters hope-filled travellers across the ancient world. Their journeys are marked by a lightness of touch and gaiety of spirit. There is nothing ordered or systematic. Mission by the Holy Spirit is not 'the planned extension of an old building', it is more like an 'unexpected explosion'.[45] The church leaders try in vain to make sense of what is happening but the Holy Spirit seems 'not to have read the rubrics'.[46] New life bursts out. 'It begins in the wounded side of Christ on Calvary, goes through the tempering of Pentecostal fires, and comes onward like a burning flood.' [47]

The urgency of mission

In the nineteenth century, missionary urgency was fuelled by the image of people falling into hell. There was a desperate need to rescue them quickly before they were lost for ever. This is not a predominant idea in the New Testament. There are references to the future plight of the wicked (Matt. 13.42; 24.51; 25.46), and a few vivid descriptions of hell (Rev. 20.10; Lk. 16.19–28), but hell as a motive for mission is largely missing from Paul, the greatest missionary of them all. Instead, missionary urgency springs from a theology of election and an understanding of *kairos*. *Kairos* is the 'elective moment' when God, through his Spirit, offers the possibility of freedom in partnership with himself (2 Cor. 6.2). Unless an immediate response is made the *kairos* moment passes. This urgency is powerfully expressed in our Lord's preaching, 'The time is fulfilled, and the kingdom of heaven is at hand; repent and believe in the gospel' (Mk 1.15). In his sending out of the twelve (Matt. 10.5–14) we again catch this sense of time running out:

> As you enter the house, salute it. And if the house is worthy, let your peace come upon it; but if it is not worthy, let your peace return to you. And if any one will not receive you or listen to your words, shake off the dust from your feet as you leave that house or town. (vv. 13–14)

These messengers travel light and carry no ideology of crusade. 'Their commission is not a heroic struggle, a fanatical pursuit of a grand idea or a good cause. That is why they stay only where the Word stays, and if it is rejected they will be rejected with it.'[48] This sense of speed comes from their wish to be identified with the dynamic Spirit of God who moves through time and space establishing networks of communication and partnership. The picture of people 'dwelling in darkness' gave urgency to mission in the nineteenth century. The idea of the 'flowing tides' of Spirit is a theological image I wish to pursue. Mission in the Holy Spirit springs from a realization that we are called to position ourselves at the 'leading edge' of history so as to celebrate the kingdom as it comes. The *kairos* moment marks the juxtaposition in time and space of God's Spirit and our 'active word', for 'we are witnesses of these things, and so is the Holy Spirit, whom God has given to those who obey him' (Acts 5.32). Thomas Merton speaks of this flowing Spirit:

God, who is everywhere, never leaves us. Yet he seems sometimes to be present, sometimes absent . . . He is like the wind that blows where it pleases. You who love him must love him as arriving from where you do not know and as going where you do not know. Your spirit must seek to be as clean and as free as his own Spirit, in order to follow him wherever he goes.[49]

Sadly we do not often obey the Spirit in this way so that much of what the Church does is not 'mission in the Holy Spirit'. The Roman Catholic, José Comblin suggests that we assume the Spirit to be present when we collect the views of theologians, publish manuals on mission, build schools, co-operatives, hospitals and hold meetings. Although the Church engages in all these can we be really sure we are doing the right things at the right time? Great discernment is required which is not a product of skill or technique but rather of listening for the Spirit:

> Living in total obedience to the Spirit does not mean trying to get an authoritative seal of approval stamped on the things that we would be doing anyway . . . Obedience to the Spirit means that we constantly refer and relate our initiative to the Spirit . . . As Jesus tells us, the Spirit is like the wind that blows where it wills.[50]

To change the metaphor; mission in the Holy Spirit is like surfing. You have to wait at the right place for the right moment – the *kairos*, and in an act of faith catch the right wave. The same process of election, which we explored in Chapter 4, is at work in the elective mission of the Holy Spirit. It is this theological understanding that produces urgency in mission for, although at times God waits or moves slowly, there are other times when he moves with such speed that huge dislocations open up in history, for the Spirit does not stay in the same place for ever and neither must we. Luther writes:

God's grace is like a passing storm of rain which does not return where once it has been . . . it came to the Jews but passed over. Paul brought it to the Greeks but it passed over . . . the Romans and Latins had it. And you must not think that you have it forever.[51]

In the present dispensation, God's enigmatic presence can surface at any time or place, and within 'any' people who, maybe without knowing it, display obedience to the partnership mandates of the covenant. The people so identified will in most cases be the marginalized and vulnerable because Jesus died outside the gate (Heb. 13.12), nailed down at the point of 'ultimate periphery'.[52] Grace is shown to be grace because it flows mainly from outside to inside, from the margins to the centre, from the poor to the rich, from the weak to the strong, from the vulnerable to the complacent (1 Cor. 1. 27–30). The Church's centre is the edge:

> The crucifixion of Jesus outside the city wall is a paschal point and a clear sign of Jesus' option for the poor. He passed over from the centre to the periphery towards those who are marginalized victims of demonic powers, political, economic, social, cultural and religious. We too must be with Jesus on the margins of society.[53]

Given the priority of Noah's covenant, particularity exists for the sake of universality. The one exists for the many. If the existing church or churches cease to display grace, gratitude and obedience to the Spirit, then the covenant God hands on the baton to some other more responsive group. God, his love for the many, frustrated by the failure of the few, continues to elect new people, inviting them into a covenant partnership with himself. Refusing to lay aside his faith in the Church, God conducts a search at the margins, creating ecclesial communities which become 'new forms' of Church.

God moves from the Tower of Babel to Pentecost, from Israel to Babylon. God moves in Europe, in Africa, in the

Americas, in Asia. As God moves, God suffers with the people, sheds tears with them, hopes with them, and creates the communion of love here and there.[54]

A *new Pentecost?*

Between 1970 and 1980 (see Chapter 3), the unpredictable winds of the Holy Spirit began to blow. The first indication that new waves of grace were on their way had been signalled in 1962 when the aged Pope John XXIII astonished the world by calling a second Vatican Council. The Roman monolith was the first church to make a realistic response to the twentieth century. By her invitation to bishops from the Third World and through her indigenization proposals, the Roman Catholic Church was demonstrating two things: that Rome was no longer the centre of the world and that the modern Church needed to open itself up again to the power of the Holy Spirit.

The second sign appeared in Geneva. The World Council of Churches, meeting at Nairobi in 1975 under the influence of Bishop Arias and then later through the advocacy of Emilio Castro, openly recognized that 'evangelism had become the Cinderella of the Church'.[55] The Council acknowledged its impotency.[56] Ordinary people did not think of Geneva as a super-ecclesial centre like Rome. The WCC could only 'assist the Churches in each place'.[57] The front line of mission was the local church. Strangely, this was the very place where the renewing power was being experienced as the tides of Spirit began to sweep across the world. Today neo-Pentecostalism has become the third ecclesiastical model of Church, as authentic as the traditional Catholic and Protestant models.

W. J. Hollenweger,[58] who has written much on Pentecostalism, believes the numerical and spiritual centre of the Christian World has now shifted, because of this movement, from the rich white West to the coloured marginalized peoples of the Third World. Through the bestowal of charismata, the empowered poor rejoice in their new identity as children of

God and, like the first messengers in the New Testament (Matt. 10.5–14), witness to their faith with bold exuberance. The flame of mission has been rekindled but the light now comes not from the rich First World but from the poor indigenous peoples of Africa, Asia and Latin America. In 1900 there were 10 million African Christians; now there are 400 million,[59] the larger percentage of these being found in the African indigenous churches.[60] Similarly in Latin America, once the bastion of Roman Catholicism, Pentecostalism has transformed the Christian landscape. It has been estimated that by 2050 only about one fifth of the world's three billion Christians will be non-Hispanic whites. The era of Western Christianity has passed within our lifetime and the day of Southern Christianity is dawning.[61]

Fourth interlude: South Africa and Malaysia

In 2001 my wife and I spent a month in the 'far country' of South Africa. It is 4.45 a.m. on a Sunday morning. We are up, before the roosters start crowing, to prepare for our 750km round trip from Johannesburg into the NW Province beyond Lichtenberg. Collected by Bishop Paul Verryn, who lives and works in Soweto, we speed along deserted roads in open stretches of farmland. In all directions, as far as the eye can see, are fields of sunflowers. As we journey the heat builds up. We are hot and sweaty by the time of our arrival at the church alongside a dusty track. There is a welcoming committee, drinks, a brightly dressed choir, groups of Manyano ladies and the inevitable gaggle of children. I shall never forget the expectant faces of that very large black congregation meeting in a sweltering hot building. As they began to sing, sway and dance, the tingles ran up and down my spine. Here was singing the like of which I had never heard before. The sound came from the heart and the body. It was soul-music refined by pain. It made me weep for joy.

After our three-hour morning service we travelled on to Kunana where Bishop Paul simply remarked, 'I was detained here.' I learnt how a few years before, the police had broken into the service and arrested him. It was only later when others spoke of his persecution, that I realized where the power and passion of his preaching came from. It came from the triumph of faith over fear. As we moved into the sharing of the bread and the wine, I looked again at the faces of the old Manyano mothers as they danced and sang. I realized why the indigenous Church of South Africa is potently alive. In their transfigured faces you saw that these poverty stricken people, who had been dehumanized by Apartheid, knew that in Christ they had received the dignity of children of God. Through this Eucharistic celebration in a wilderness place a new rainbow world was anticipated.

Another cameo, this time from the 'far country' of Malaysia. In 1989 I was invited to preach at various places and to lead Bible Studies on renewal in a hotel in Malacca. The powerful resurgence of Islam followed by the ban on any propagation of the gospel among the main indigenous people, the Malays, had restricted the activities of Christians and raised acute theological questions about how one could evangelize. Christians are a small minority, only 6 per cent of the total population. Many were afraid and a few had friends who had been imprisoned for their faith. During my time in this 'far country' I kept wondering whether I might get thrown out, or worse.[62]

The convention had been set up to give Bible teaching to Methodists and others who had experienced the renewing power of the Holy Spirit. I found people hungry for the Word and bursting with faith and life. During worship, on the Saturday evening following Easter, I sensed that what I had prepared was not right. What should I do? I distinctly recall flicking anxiously through my Bible until my attention was drawn to 1 Kings 19.18, 'Yet I will leave seven thousand in Israel, all the knees that have not bowed to Baal.' It was not a promising text yet it grabbed me. For the next 30 minutes I listened to myself speak of the way in which God attempted to convert Elijah to a new way of understanding by reminding him of God's hidden work. 'Now is the day of small things, the secret silent God is at work in history, do you see, do you hear that still small voice? . . . It is in weakness, brokenness and obedience that we bear our witness.' As I was speaking, slowly in ones and twos, the people began to come out and kneel waiting for ministry. Moved to silence, I knelt and joined them, awaiting that deeper ministry of God's Spirit.[63]

The Holy Spirit like a mighty wind is blowing through the nations. Grace is flowing from the edge to the centre. The peoples of the Third World, especially the marginalized and the poor, are experiencing this renewing life. In their presence one can only kneel in repentance. They have become the means of grace for those of us who, like the elder brother in the story of the lost son, find it difficult to join in the music and the dancing.

7

From decline to growth

Church growth depends on winning converts. Churches grow from nothing but converts – people who believe on Jesus Christ intensely enough to break with their past sins and cleave to Him as Lord and Saviour. Converts are not picked up lying loose on the beach. They are won by men and women whose own beliefs blaze hot enough to kindle faith in others.[1]

Malaysia, like other former British colonies, was a place where a little bit of England was re-enacted in the churches. Dramatic growth in the Church only occurred after the Brits had left.[2] It is estimated that in Malaysia and Singapore there are now about 75 million Christians in the new 'cell churches'. I recall an early morning Easter Communion, celebrated by a layperson, in the villa of one of the members. The numbers in this cell had grown to 18, three times over in the past four years, enabling it to split in half like an amoeba to form two new cells. As the sun rose we prayed, praised and greeted the risen Christ. This would be their last occasion of worshipping together in this home. There was much to celebrate. They had experienced edification and multiplication through the Spirit.

I have already described some indigenous models of Church: the Saccidananda Ashram, the Subaseth Gedara community, the vibrant African congregation and the Malaysian cell church. In each case most of the European cultural trappings had been abandoned, theology and liturgy reshaped, and the nineteenth-century iron cage of institution and structure broken open. These churches have little ecclesiastical red tape or built-in obsolescence. Inculturation has taken place. They have become churches 'outside the box'[3] and 'on the edge'. In this and the chapters which follow, I am adopting Peter Hodgson's definition of Church (p. 60) and referring to these new forms of Church as 'ecclesial communities'.

Decline and growth

In Britain, 'the Church is increasingly in danger of being left high and dry as one of the last bastions of modernity. In organizational terms, it is arguable that the mainline denominations are already the last modernist, Victorian bureaucracies that are left.'[4] One senses that the aging congregations, who attend the mainline churches, are still nostalgically attempting to perpetuate the Sunday School church of their childhood. For many the modern world is the 'far country'. In 1979, the Nationwide Initiative in Evangelism produced a statistical evaluation of the churches in England. The results were disturbing; church members made up only 18 per cent of the population.[5] Frustrated ministers began to look for strategies which might reverse this relentless decline. 'Church growth' was heralded as a possible answer. Donald McGavran (1897–1990) was its prophet.

Born in India and coming from a family of missionaries, McGavran spent 31 years as a missionary, becoming an expert in education and the organization of medical work. In 1954 he returned to the United States disappointed at not seeing any significant numerical increase in church-going during his whole ministry. He had observed that while the 'Church of the poor' was expanding at an exponential rate, the more traditional 'Western churches' both in the Third World and more especially in Europe and America were declining. Why is it, he asked, that 7,600 people in Europe and North America are being lost daily, while Africa is making 16,400 new Christians[6] every day? Why, he asked, given the same devotedness, prayer and faith by evangelist and people, do some churches grow while others do not? As far back as 1933 he had puzzled over this. In 1955 he produced an answer in his trail-blazing book, *The Bridges of God*.[7]

Retiring in 1961, McGavran opened the Institute of Church Growth in Oregon and later became founding Dean of the School of World Mission at the Fuller Theological Institute at Pasadena. Through extensive research, the examination of case-studies and by using the tools of sociology and anthropology, McGavran and his disciples were able, in many different contexts, to identify receptive peoples so successfully that 'church growth' has become both a prescriptive and a predictive science.

The great commission: make disciples

We in the West have become so accustomed to declining churches that we no longer believe in the possibility of numerical growth. We cling to remnant theologies or modify our counting procedures to avoid the painful truth. We comfort ourselves by saying, 'quality is to be preferred to quantity', or 'God is more interested in reducing numbers than increasing them'. McGavran rigorously dispels all these false theological rationalizations of non-growth, arguing that we must again make evangelism our top priority.[8] He does not overlook the social or political dimension but argues that 'our social causes will not triumph unless we have great numbers of committed Christians'.[9]

The only way to cut through the confusion of current debates about mission, says McGavran, is to return to the 'great commission'. Mission is God's mission and mission is evangelism.[10] Evangelism is the activity of witnessing, converting and incorporating new Christians into the Church. It is summed up in the word 'discipling'. Appealing to the parables of the lost sheep, the lost coin, and the lost son, he states, 'mere search is not what God wants. God wants his lost children found' (Lk. 19.10). The task of mission is a 'vast and purposeful finding'.[11] Like the shepherd in the parable, we should count the sheep since numerical growth in membership must be 'regarded as a chief consideration in estimating church welfare'.[12]

His exposition of the 'great commission' is imaginative. He suggests, first, that Matthew 28.18–20 outlines the missionary method to be employed. The verb 'disciple' (*matheteusate*), in the imperative mood, is explained by the two participles, 'baptizing' and 'teaching'. These actions, says McGavran, describe the two stages of discipling. We secure a first commitment by baptizing receptive people. Once the newly baptized are within the life of the Church the 'perfecting process' through teaching can begin.

Drawing on the research of Rolf Winter, McGavran secondly interprets Matthew's 'all the nations' (*panta ta ethne*) as a series of sociological mosaics which he calls 'homogeneous units' (HUs). While faith flows relatively easily across a particular piece of the mosaic, it always stops at the edge. The boundary is a place of linguistic, cultural or ethnic change. Different pieces of the mosaic become receptive at different times through the elective work of God's Spirit and by their interaction with surrounding pieces. People rapidly become Christian, he found, 'when least change of race or clan is involved'.[13] He concludes, 'people like to become Christians without crossing racial, linguistic or class barriers'. McGavran says that the first years of the Church's history illustrate this homogeneous principle. At the beginning those who became Christians managed to retain their membership of the Jewish community. Problems only arose when attempts were made to integrate Jewish Christians with Hellenistic Christians. The main difficulty was therefore not theological but social.[14] However, 'the creation of narrow Churches, selfishly centered on the salvation of their own kith and kin only, is never the goal'.[15] Recognizing Paul's vision that all are one in Jesus Christ (Gal. 3.28) and committed as he is to the homogeneous principle, McGavran argues that the integration of the various homogeneous units should be addressed later in the perfecting stage.

Questions about church growth

McGavran's disciples have produced a steady stream of books combining 'church growth' methods with management technique. Business plans are drawn up. Numbers become the criterion. Christianity becomes a commodity to be marketed.[16] One book suggests that a correct method of ministry 'reaches the immediate objective with the greatest efficiency in the expenditure of resources and energies'.[17] Wagner turns 'church growth' into a programme of ministerial management which 'helps us to maximize the use of energy and other resources for God's greater glory'.[18] If this is how God wants us to work, what are we to make of the gracious act of the woman who inefficiently wasted her precious ointment on Jesus (Matt. 26.7)? The management 'numbers game' does not spring from a theology of the covenant God but rather reflects one of the mechanistic preoccupations of Western middle-class males.

While Luke does a lot of counting, Paul commends the Thessalonian Christians, not because their numbers have increased, but because they have retained their integrity through suffering, becoming 'imitators of us and of the Lord' (1 Thess. 1.6). Hans-Ruedi Weber therefore wonders if God's way of counting is the same as McGavran's. 'God's arithmetic', he says, 'uses representative numbers not actual figures.'[19] Is numerical growth always healthy? One writer from Latin America has suggested that churches with increasing numbers may not be growing 'up' at all (1 Cor. 3.1–2), they may simply be growing 'fat'.[20] Numerical growth is only healthy when it is accompanied by growth in other areas of spirituality: outreach, 'biblical and theological depth, and the struggle for peace and justice'.[21] Should not the numerical size of a Christian community be related to the context in which it is situated and to the missionary task required of it? This is ably demonstrated by the examples of the Saccidananda Ashram and the Subaseth Gedara communities. Churches are not meant to be monochrome if inculturation is taken seriously. They ought rather to replicate contextually the diversity, colour and variety of the incarnational, rainbow God of covenant.

What about the 'homogeneous principle' and the assumption that, in the perfecting phase, several homogeneous churches can be integrated through a catechetical programme? The Chicago theologian, James Gustafson, suggests that this is not easily achieved. Because many such churches reflect the questionable values of the society in which they are placed, the numerically stronger tend to inflict their cultural norms on the weaker.[22] The sociologist, Wayne McClintock, thinks McGavran makes dubious use of the social sciences.[23] He argues that McGavran's sociology lacks precision in the treatment of social boundaries, assumes a static interpretation of history and therefore does not adequately describe the complex process of social change. McGavran therefore underestimates the strength of the economic and political elitist forces at work within society. Writing from the Latin American experience, Orlando Costas observes that McGavran fails to take account of the oppressive power of corporate human wickedness because his theological understanding of structural sin is defective. Expansion in the Latin American context, Costas concludes, was brought about by 'aggressive denominational competition' which has generated distrust and been blind to injustice.[24] Robin Gill, examining the British scene, points to evidence suggesting that successful Christians always want to dominate the less successful.[25] If there is truth in this barrage of criticism, then 'church growth' theory can produce Christian communities which, like Israel of old (see Chapter 4) fail to act justly by exchanging their vocation as vulnerable servant for one of mastery and control.

So where does 'church growth' fit within the *missio Dei*? Orlando Costas suggests we must not ask, what is the Church's 'primary' task, instead the question is, what is the Church's 'total' task?[26] 'Church growth' has to be viewed in a holistic way.[27] He defines four dimensions. First, there is 'numerical' expansion which we have already mentioned. Second, there is 'organic' expansion. This describes the structural and organizational shape of the Church as a community of faith. The structure should be flexible enough in its development to take account both of the context in which it is placed and of the changing dynamic of the Spirit's mission. Third, there is 'conceptual' expansion. Christians should not grow fat or behave like spiritual babies (1 Cor. 3.1): they must 'in all things grow up' (Eph. 4.14–16). If there is no theological, emotional and spiritual development then, despite numerical increase, the Church is not growing. Fourth, there is 'incarnational' expansion. This relates to the degree in which the Church is participating 'in the afflictions of her world, her prophetic, intercessory, and liberating action on behalf of the weak and destitute; the intensity of her preaching to the poor, the brokenhearted, the captives, the blind, and the oppressed' (Lk. 4. 18–21).[28]

Despite the deficiencies of 'church growth', Costas argues that one of the most important contributions is the way in which the 'church growth movement' challenges the decline and pessimism of churches and inspires an 'optimistic forward-looking approach to the missionary enterprise'.[29]

McGavran and Methodism

John Wesley records his visit to Newgate, Bristol, on 26 and 27 April 1739:

> In the evening I was again pressed in spirit to declare, that 'Christ gave Himself a ransom for all'. And almost before we called upon Him to set His seal, He answered. One was so wounded by the sword of the Spirit, that you would have imagined she could not live a moment. But immediately His abundant kindness was showed, and she loudly sang of His righteousness.
>
> All Newgate rang with the cries of those whom the Word of God cut to the heart: two of whom were in a moment filled with joy, to the astonishment of those that beheld them.[30]

Both McGavran and Wesley emphasize the need for confidence and dependence on the Holy Spirit. McGavran says that effective witnesses need a 'burning faith'.[31] The hymns of Charles Wesley bear witness to the conviction, faith and enthusiasm which fired the first Methodists.[32] In the Malaysian 'cell church' and in some of the South African congregations, the same exuberant energy is to be found. People today, as in the New Testament, are deeply affected by the contagion of the Spirit.[33] Confidence in the gospel is even more necessary in our Western pluralist society.[34] McGavran encouraged nominal Christians to be baptized with the Holy Spirit, for only then would they become passionate advocates of the gospel. John Wesley also believed this, though he expressed it differently. He regarded nominal Christians as little different from pagans.[35] He instructed his lay preachers, 'You have nothing to do but to save souls. Therefore spend and be spent in this work. And go always, not to those that want you, but to those that want you most.'[36]

Second, both stress the importance of ongoing discipleship. McGavran's definition of evangelism as the making of disciples integrates the activity of witness, the creation of obedient disciples and the planting of new churches. 'Faithfulness in proclamation and finding is not enough. There must be faithful aftercare.'[37] John Wesley held that awakening people without enfolding them into redemptive cells does more harm than good. He, too, argued that the awakened must be trained quickly in the ways of God.[38] Because disciples are disciplined people, converts were placed in classes under supervision and given a rule to live by. Wesley's method of teaching was designed to enable members to 'do good'. His 'methodical' process of formation, similar to that practised in 'cell churches', produced a rapidly growing body of adherents. In 1768, Methodism had 27,341 members; in 1778, the figure was 40,089; a decade later 66,375; and by 1798 there were 101,712 members. This is the stuff of burning faith and obedience.[39]

Third, they both believed that 'the poor' were the best

evangelists. McGavran is troubled by the problem of 'lift'. When people from poor areas become Christians and join the Church, they begin to have victory over laziness, vice and ignorance. In acquiring status and some measure of education they begin to desire better things for themselves and their family. The fellowship of the Church 'lifts' them from one social class to another. This, however, has a negative effect. In developing new tastes, in embracing a different value system and in forging new friendships, the young Christian becomes separated from his former less sophisticated associates. McGavran rightly asks, how can we prevent goodness and education from creating separation? [40] The sons of Zebedee, says McGavran, may have left their nets, but they did not give up being fishermen. Likewise the first Jewish Christians did not cease to be Jews.[41] By insisting on the rapid training of new converts which turns them quickly into leaders and evangelists, the danger of lift is reduced.[42] Wesley modelled Methodism's mission from his reading of the Acts of the Apostles, where the first messengers were ordinary people, fired by the Spirit. Methodism was a movement mostly among the poor. With virtually no ordained clergy at his disposal, every member had to be a missionary. Evangelism, as the priority, was pursued regardless of formal church order. George Hunter sums up Wesley's vision:

> The identity of the church is located in its apostolic mission and ministry to people (and to whole populations) who are not yet people of faith, and this ministry and mission are primarily entrusted to the laity.[43]

The answer lies in the soil

Churches grow better in some sociological contexts rather than in others. Since the Spirit constantly seeks to incarnate the Word into a culture, the '*kairos* of the Spirit' is not unrelated to the '*kairos* of the culture'. McGavran investigates this relationship in his teaching about 'fields':

Our Lord spoke of fields in which the seed had just been sown and of those ripe for harvest . . . Our Lord took account of the varying ability of individuals and societies to hear and obey the Gospel . . . Unevenness of growth has marked the church from the beginning. The common people, the Gospels tell us, received our Lord's message better than the Pharisees and Sadducees . . . One thing is clear – receptivity wanes as often as it waxes. Like the tide, it comes in and goes out. Unlike the tide, no one can guarantee when it goes out and that it will come back.[44]

Because there is a time for sowing, a time for waiting, a time for pruning and a time for harvesting it is important to discern the *kairos* of the Spirit. This enables us through an examination of the 'fields' (Lk. 13.6–9) to distribute resources appropriately, plan strategies correctly and interpret theologically what God is doing.

In the first century there was a combination of cultural and sociological factors which aided the rapid expansion of Christianity.[45] It was a time of peace. There was a superb network of well-maintained roads, the like of which had never been seen before nor would be seen again for over a thousand years. The message could therefore be carried rapidly from city to city by a mobile population of Christian soldiers and slaves (Acts 8.4). There was one common Greek language which could be understood in most places across the empire. The culture was generally homogenous. Roman cities had a similar social structure, lay-out and organization. The same model of evangelism could therefore be used again and again to great effect. Because the Roman concept of 'household' (*oikonomia*) was an extended hierarchical family, if the 'head' became a Christian then all members of the family would become Christians (1 Cor. 1.16). Paul's Roman citizenship gave him sufficient status to enter freely into these well-to-do households.[46] Finally, Christianity appeared on the scene at a time when the ancient cults and religions were tired and spiritually bankrupt. In short, the *kairos* of the culture with its solidarity, homogeneity and excellent communications was ripe for the contagious spread of the gospel.

In the sixteenth century the message of the Protestant Reformation was carried swiftly across Europe on the wings of the printing presses. The spread of Methodism was aided in the eighteenth century by the introduction of cheap printing and the lighting of city streets after dark, enabling people to attend evening meetings in relative safety. In the great missionary century which followed, the development of the telegraph and powerful steam locomotion by rail and sea facilitated a rapid global expansion of Christianity and Western culture.[47] Today the advanced communications technology of the Western world ought to enable the growth of the Western Church, yet it has not happened. Why is this?

First, in tribal societies, where there is a sense of solidarity or *ubuntu*, whole families are baptized at the same time. In the post-modern individualistic culture of Europe and North America, the contagion of the Spirit spreads from one person to the next rather than through corporate groups. So individuals only trickle into the Church because they have to be converted one by one and not as extended families. Further, in many Third World countries the migration of people from rural areas to cities, in recent years, has detached them from their traditional religious and tribal structures so making them more receptive to the gospel.[48] Second, Christians in the West like to keep control. McGavran, taking up the insights of Roland Allen, argues that local people should take responsibility as soon as possible.[49] This is not easy for us.[50] Our history of empire building has conditioned us to keep people in a relationship of dependence. Moreover, we have a detached, 'professional view' of leadership which often inhibits the emergence of new untried leaders at the local level. Third, Christianity in the First World is mostly concerned with the private, the spiritual and the social, having separated itself from the political aspects of life. Such a peripheral, self-absorbing culture has less impact on society at large.

Fourth, the British have a sentimental attachment to church

buildings which they seldom enter, and are proud of ecclesiastical institutions which they no longer respect. Chronic over-building in the nineteenth century has been one of the factors in causing a decline of church membership in the twentieth.[51] Sadly, much of our churchgoing population has still not got beyond the Enid Blyton Book of Bible Stories.[52] The mainline churches with their top-heavy, old-fashioned institutions and managed structures have become 'no-go' areas for the majority of our population. McGavran's exposition of the 'homogeneous unit' reminds us that the cultural life of a particular church must relate and resonate with the cultural existence of the people it is trying to attract. If British churches are to grow, then a radical reappraisal of our internal, theological, linguistic, social, ethnic, organizational and liturgical activities must be undertaken.

The answer lies in the Spirit

In 1988 the Bishop of Hyderabad included in his keynote address to the Lambeth Conference, the story of how the gospel was first brought to his people by an English doctor who set up a small clinic in one of the villages:

> The people said, 'The English have failed to conquer us with their army so they are now trying to poison us with this man's medicine.' No one went to the clinic. After some weeks a dog with a broken leg wandered in and the doctor, having time on his hands, cleaned the wound, bound it up with a splint and sent the dog on its way. The people watched the dog and said to one another, 'If this man is so good as to heal a worthless creature like a dog, then perhaps he will be good for us.' The bishop concluded the story by saying that was how the people came to faith; then he asked, 'Who was the real missionary to my people? It was the dog who witnessed to where he found healing. I call this "dogology".'[53]

I call this 'the mystery of the Holy Spirit' since God uses strange and unexpected ways to evangelize. There is always an indefinable element in trying to determine why and how a particular church grows. Channels or methods which have proved effective in one context can become barriers in another. Something which assumes importance in one place can act as an imported irrelevance elsewhere.

Peter Cotterell tells of the Kimbanguist Church started by Simon Kimbangu in the early twentieth century. This energetic church has spread across a dozen countries in Africa and continues to grow at a phenomenal rate not unlike the eighteenth-century expansion of the Methodism movement. This African prophetic movement holds lightly to Western concerns about credal statements, clericalism, the Eucharist, the status of polygamists, head-covering, feminism and a host of topics.[54] It focuses instead on issues we have de-mythologized like demonology, exorcisms and healing. It is an African church led by Africans, preached by Africans and thoroughly inculturated into the soil of Africa. Whatever the insights of 'church growth' we must never forget that the Holy Spirit is the principal agent of evangelization.[55] We must also be careful not to grieve the Spirit by working to our agenda and not to his.

The Church of the poor

McGavran like Wesley believed that missionary effort should focus on the marginalized. There has been a tendency, in some missionary circles, to deprecate mass missionary movements amongst the poor.[56] Evangelize the classes and they will evangelize the masses. In fact the converse is true.[57] Professor John De Gruchy from South Africa argues that the future of the Church in South Africa lies in its willingness to establish solidarity with the poor indigenous churches in the townships. Only then will the institutional Church be transformed.[58]

McGavran recognized that the poor are always more receptive to the Spirit than the rich (Lk. 6.20). For the dispossessed in the war-torn countries of Africa, and in the cities of Latin America and Asia, the gospel is welcomed as 'good news' bringing dignity and hope. We in the rich First World, enslaved by our own consumerist propaganda, are too busy worshipping the secularized god of mammon. John Wesley maintained that one cannot know or serve Christ without friendship with the poor; indeed he considered the poor to be a 'means of grace'.[59]

Theodore Jennings Jr. in his important essay 'Good News to the Poor in the Wesleyan Heritage'[60] argues that Wesley turned away from the prosperous and sought out the poor, visiting them, living with them, begging on their behalf and continually seeking their welfare. When Wesley spoke of stewardship he was not talking about fund-raising for a middle-class institution. He was talking about the redistribution of wealth from the prosperous to the poor.[61] Jesus brings good news, but it is not good news for all in the same way. It is good news for the poor and disturbing news for the rich. Wesley believed that Methodism should retain its roots amongst the poor. His great fear was that his 'societies' would become middle-class, which is precisely what happened. If the Church becomes prosperous it will still exist but only as a dead sect 'having the form of religion without the power'.[62] Separation from the poor is separation from the triune God. This suggests a portentous relocation of the 'sign of the divine' from the 'inside' to the 'outside' so that the 'vulnerable other' becomes the 'transcendent other'.[63]

We in the West, seduced by 'the market', live with the illusion that we are free, while those who cannot afford this fantasy of liberty are physically oppressed and driven to the margins.[64] Globalization, however, has now made talk of First and Third Worlds obsolete as violence, fragmentation and exclusion increase 'within' countries and not just between them.[65] It is therefore paramount that the Western Church listens both to the marginalized within its own borders as well as to the indigenous poor of Africa, Latin America, Asia and the Middle East. Only in solidarity with the marginalized will we be liberated from the idolatrous grip of consumerism and individualism, and discover new models of mission through which the God of grace can renew us all.

From the far country

Harvey Cox, who beguiled us in the sixties with his *The Secular City*, argues in his recent book, *Fire from Heaven*, that Pentecostalism rather than secularism will shape the future life of the Church.[66] There are at present some 500 million Pentecostalists scattered across the globe. This ever expanding expression of Church comes from the edge to challenge the centre. It comes from the poor to rebuke the rich.

The future of Christianity undoubtedly lies in the 'far country' rather than in Europe and North America. As John Mbiti has observed, the centres of the Church's universality are no longer Geneva, Rome, Athens, Paris, London and New York but Kinshasa, Buenos Aires, Addis Ababa and Manila.[67] The Holy Spirit is calling us in the First World to make a radical reappraisal of our understanding and practice of mission. The Roman Catholic theologian Karl Rahner, checking the pulse of the Church after the second Vatican Council, says that this shift will be similar to the one which took place in the first and second centuries when Jewish Christianity became Hellenistic. European Christianity, he says, has now to be transformed into a 'World Christianity'.[68] Johann Metz, also from Germany, recognizes the same short epoch of Jewish Christianity which contained only one cultural strand. Then, he says, comes a long epoch consisting of several strands within a single European culture until finally today we enter the era of a 'culturally polycentric universal Church'. Theologians from the Third World also refer to three stages in the Church's missionary development. Carlos Abesamis, from the Philippines, speaks of a Semitic stage, a Greek stage and a third stage marked by the advent of liberation theology. Bimweni, from Zaire, charts a similar course, his first landmark being the Jerusalem Council which produced a Church of the Gentiles, then comes the collapse of the colonial system in the middle of the last century, and this opens up the possibility of a new type of World Church.

These voices sing one song. The Western Church has to come to terms with the 'new paradigm' which, according to Tissa Balasuriya, will be the most important theological innovation since the Protestant Reformation.[69] This paradigm shift invites us to feast at the same table in the wilderness with those who have a faith which is different from our own. It calls us to embrace expressions of Christianity which may be uncongenial to us.

James Laney in his reflections on Ephesians 2.11–22 says:

> When we look back at the history of the Church, every time we see that the Church has become captive to the dominant identity of its society, every time it has become comfortable with its role in culture, it has lost its universality. With the loss of universality, it has lost the power to create, not merely to evangelize, but also the power to become renewed . . . [70]

The Western Church can be renewed when it again establishes its universality through global partnerships with the poor. The Holy Spirit seeks to bring together those who are far off and those who are near so that we are no longer strangers but fellow citizens (Eph. 2.13–14). The necessity of global partnerships between churches at all levels follows directly from our consideration of covenants. In Luke's parable of the two sons (Lk. 15.11–32) the Father wants a relationship of grace and gratitude to exist between them. Jesus gives us another parable referring to the 'far county' (Lk. 19.11–27). A nobleman goes into the 'far country' to receive kingly power and gives assets to each of his servants before leaving. On his return he rewards those at home who have taken risks, but those who have played it safe lose even what they have.

We in the prosperous West must risk all, and turn to the Church in the 'far country' which may again be able to teach

us the meaning of grace and gratitude, brokenness and blessing. In this new relationship we are no longer the triumphalis-
tic sending Church, we are to be the learning Church, humbly
seeking to discover what we have lost. The fascinating feature
of such a partnership is that we do not know what we have
lost until we discover it among the poor. In the 'far country' I
stumbled across this 'treasure in a field'. Through partnerships
in prayer, by exchanges of both personnel and information,
God can open us up by his Holy Spirit to new possibilities of
being Church.

The Holy Spirit disturbs us in order to renew us. She grieves
over our blindness, is present to our wounds, transcends this
world of violence, touches the scars of the earth and embraces
the black holes of the cosmos. She is ever watchful lest the
watery chaos overwhelm us. She searches out the dislocations
in our culture seeking to restore balance and reconnecting
what is broken. She is the preserver of life in every storm, the
promise of light in the darkest hour. Hyun Kyung's sermon in
the Canberra Assembly of World Churches, 1991, challenges
all bigotry and unconnectedness:

> Dear sisters and brothers, with the energy of the Spirit let us
> tear apart all walls of division and the culture of death
> which separates us. Let us participate in the Holy Spirit's
> economy of life, fighting for our life on this earth, in solid-
> arity with all living beings . . .Wild wind of the Holy Spirit
> blow to us. Let us welcome her, letting ourselves go in her
> wild rhythm of life. Come Holy Spirit, renew the whole of
> creation.[71]

Returning home

8

What is mission?
Coming to the Father

So he went and hired himself out to a citizen of that country, who sent him to his fields to feed pigs. He longed to fill his stomach with the pods that the pigs were eating, but no-one gave him anything. When he came to his senses, he said, 'How many of my father's hired men have food to spare, and here I am starving to death! I will set out and go back to my father and say to him: Father, I have sinned against heaven and against you. I am no longer worthy to be called your son; make me like one of your hired men.' So he got up and went to his father. (Lk. 15.15–20)

This book attempts to answer two related questions, 'what is mission?' and 'what is the God of mission like?' I suggested, in Chapter 2, that God is like an author writing a novel. We have now learnt that the title of the novel is 'The *Missio Dei*', and the story is to be enacted in the theatre of the world. Chapter 1 set the scene with its painted backdrop of Matthew's 'great commission' and Luke's parable of 'the lost son'. In subsequent chapters various players move onto the stage: Noah trailing the rainbow covenant, Abraham responding to the election of God, Jesus breaking the bread and pouring out the wine of the Spirit. These, and their understudies, enact the drama of the Trinitarian God who opens his arms to embrace humankind as partners in the renewal and restoration of all things. We, the audience, are invited on to the stage to participate in the story and to be present with the cast on their tour of the 'far country'. The experience is revelatory. At our homecoming we will at last be able to 'see the Father', the author of this wonderful epic of redemption.

The God of mission

What is the God of mission like? He is the fountain of sending love.[1] He is the God of grace, who chooses to limit himself and embrace us in a covenant partnership. He is the God who, experiencing the violence of his troubled world, makes himself accountable for all that takes place (Gen. 6.6).[2] He is the God who listens and comes down into our world bringing liberation, hope and healing to the poor and the oppressed (Ex. 3.7). He is the God who listens to our laments and learns from the protests and the petitions of the vulnerable.[3] She is the God who like a mother hen seeks to gather her brood under her wings for protection (Matt. 23.37). She is the God who processes the pain within herself as she continues to renew the covenant relationship between us. This is the God who seeks his own liberation in the salvation of the cosmos. This God is no metaphysical creation of the philosophers; this is the living God of the Bible. This is the God of miracle in whom hurt and hope so coalesce as to bring about the redemption of all things. This is the God of brokenness and blessing; the God who evokes grace and gratitude in his people. This is the God of the universal and the particular, the God who sends waves of Spirit rippling through the universe.

The rainbow sign is God's sure reminder that he ever continues his work of preserving and sustaining creation. If there are places where he is absent (Ps. 139.7–8) then those regions of the cosmos would collapse back into the nothingness from which they were taken. This preserving and renewing maintenance work is hidden from us. Martin Luther wrote of God as both 'hidden' and 'revealed' (*Deus Absconditus* and *Deus Revelatus*). One of the properties of God is his 'hiddenness'.[4] Human beings, argues Luther, would be overwhelmed by the nakedness of God.[5] His presence is hidden in cloud, and even Moses, who penetrates the cloud, does not see God's face.

The New Testament, through its use of the word 'mystery' (*mysterion*), forbids all questions which seek to probe the hiddenness of God. To speculate is to fall into idolatry[6] and invent a fictitious God. Luther, following the New Testament, is strident in his criticisms of theologies of this sort. Instead we are called to live by faith and not by sight. Through the process of election, God chooses to make some of his hidden work visible to the eye of faith. Yet this is not straightforward, for even here God wears a mask.

In the present age of the Spirit we view truth by means of a mirror, enigmatically (1 Cor. 13.12).[7] The God who reveals himself is not simply 'wholly other' but 'completely different' from what we might expect.[8] The God who chooses the way of covenant shows himself as one who having laid aside the 'form of God' (*forma Dei*), takes the 'form of a servant' (*forma servi*) (Phil. 2.6f.). Within this form there is no 'flashing through' of some extra divinity other than the incarnational form assumed. With this covenant God there is no God, as it were, behind the back of God. The 'form of God' has been renounced. God comes to us in the form of weakness, vulnerability and condescension. This servant form was meant to be reflected in Israel. Because of their failure it became perfectly replicated in Jesus Christ who, through the baptism of the Spirit, enables this revelation to be reproduced in the children of Abraham who are of the Spirit and not of the flesh (Gal. 3.2–9). This God of covenant 'can assume the form of weakness and do so as omnipotence triumphing in this form'.[9] So in the present dispensation of the Spirit, grace flows from the weak to the strong, from the vulnerable to the self-sufficient; not the other way round. For the foolishness of God is wiser than men, and the weakness of God is stronger than men (1 Cor. 1.25). Thus the mystery which is revealed to us is that for God it is just as natural 'to be lowly as it is to be high, to be near as it is to be far, to be little as it is to be great, to be abroad as to be at home'.[10]

Our theology of the God of mission is encapsulated in our Lord's parable of the two sons (Lk. 15.11–32). The loving father lets his younger son depart but holds on to the relationship between them. Although the father stays at home, his pain-love follows the son into the 'far country'. 'The eyes that searched for and finally caught sight of the son in the distance tell of a heart that was with the son.'[11] It is the father's abiding invitation to return and the son's memory of a gracious father which finally lures him home.

The Trinitarian God of covenant has so bound himself to fallen humanity that inclusive relationships take precedence over contractual rules. Neither of the two sons understands this. The younger regards himself as 'no longer worthy' and therefore only deserves to be welcomed back as a 'hired hand'. The older brother might have been prepared to accept him on these terms which are the conventional rules for responsible behaviour. The father, however, will have none of this. His embrace, the gifts of robe, ring and feast transformed the lost son into a 'son-to-be-proud-of'. Because grace is uncondi- tional, no confession was necessary before the embrace. This parable seems to negate the possibility of ultimate exclusion. Does this mean therefore, that there is no eternal damnation? The answer to this question is left hanging in the air and unre- solved because the story ends with the elder brother 'outside'. But he is outside 'with' the Father who now joins him there.

Who is this strange father? He is certainly not a sentimental old man who cannot let go.[12] Although relationships are placed before rules, justice does not disappear in the face of mercy. The father does not destroy law, or overturn the struc- tures of society, instead he 're-orders' the order by setting inclusion before exclusion.[13] Both sons are treated justly. The father does not reinstate the younger son to all the former privileges since he gets no second inheritance. Neither does the elder son miss out, for all that the father has is now his and will come to him (v. 31). Justice is done, but in the context of grace. Both are sons of the father, and both are always 'with him' even when they go into their own respective 'far countries'; the younger as he seeks to carve out a new identity for himself in a distant place, the elder standing outside in the father's backyard trapped in his own self-righteousness. The younger is 'my son who was lost and is found' and the elder is 'my son' who has yet to embrace his brother. Christian mission can therefore no longer be set in exclusive theologies which invariably culminate in the reality of hell. Rather, hell now stands for the possibility of our excluding ourselves by our exclusion of others. God excludes nobody. The 'trembling gates of hell' have now been shaken by the Trinitarian God who places relationships before rules and embrace before exclusion.

What mission is not

Many of us have inherited, through the hymns of the late nineteenth century, the idea that the purpose of mission is to 'save souls' or 'win the world for Christ' or 'bring salvation to the heathen'.[14] Most evangelicals with an exclusive theology have similar aims but now approach the missionary task in a refined and sensitive way.[15] Others blindly rush in with less sophistication.[16] Missionaries have taken and still take, inappropriate cultural and theological baggage with them.[17] Yet although mistakes are made we cannot doubt their passion.[18] Missionary stories are marked by blessing and brokenness; the costly sacrifice of some is the stuff of legend.[19]

We saw, in Chapter 3, that the utopian dream of evangelizing the world was carried over into the twentieth century and given confident re-expression in the Edinburgh Missionary Conference of 1910. Of the 1,200 delegates present only 17 came from 'other lands'. The representation at the World Mission Conference in San Antonio, 79 years later, was profoundly different.[20] Of the 649 delegates, 70 per cent came from non-European and non-American countries and 44 per cent were women. The centre of World Christianity has shifted decisively, and this must radically affect our interpretation of the missionary task.

First, the destructive ravages of the twentieth century have made Christians either more holistic or more apocalyptic. For the latter, an unbridgeable chasm opens up between this world and the next. Apocalyptic responses spawn dangerous theologies of violence and exclusion rather than embrace. I have argued that this approach must be confronted and resisted. If mission is set in a holistic framework then our task can no longer be conceived as 'saving souls'. This notion, a product of Western reductionism and fragmentation, fails in its anthropological description of persons. A human 'soul' cannot be separated out from the complexity of the human personality which is formed as much by physical, genetic, sociological and environmental factors as by decisions of each individual human will. The rainbow covenant suggests that we only properly understand ourselves as persons by giving due regard to our relationships with others and to our symbiotic relationship with the rest of creation. This more corporate understanding challenges the rampant individualism of the First World.

Second, the resurgence and advance of other religions suggests that 'dialogue' rather than 'crusade' is now a more appropriate model for evangelism. Dialogue already helps us to see that 'salvation' is a very slippery word. In different contexts it can mean different things. A Buddhist might interpret salvation as an experience of illumination, a Hindu as union with God, an alcoholic as deliverance from drink, a starving man will regard it as an offer of bread.[21] We have to be careful not to impose our own concept of 'salvation' on to people whose world-view is different from ours. Yet salvation remains the essential task of mission (a definition of this will be given in the next section).

Third, knowing the treasure of the gospel to be contained in earthen vessels (2 Cor. 4.7) we now recognize that cultural assumptions affect every re-presentation of the gospel. These accretions can distort the substance of the message just as the world-view of the recipients affects the 'hearing' of the message. We must take on board the insights we have learnt about inculturation and the challenge of cross-cultural evangelism.[22]

Fourth, today we live in a global village where different faiths and ideologies can either coexist or compete against one another. The very notion of 'winning the world' becomes very questionable and even dangerous. The 'nations' of the world are not passive anthropological groupings of pagans waiting to be converted. Such an assumption not only shows a marked lack of respect for people but masks an inherent racism. Conversion certainly is one of the aims of mission. It must not, however, be understood as simply getting a group of people, who are different from us, to believe the same things as we do and become like us. Denton Lotz, in his article on 'Peter's Wider Understanding of God's Will', says:

> Humankind and its many religions fall into the temptation of making the universal God of all a particular god of the few. In other words, we make God into a tribal deity . . . Religion, speaking negatively, strengthens the taboos and prejudices of a society. In preserving the identity of a group, it at the same time isolates and condemns that which is different, that which is outside the group.[23]

Finally, we are not attempting to 'bring salvation' to the nations. In Chapter 2, we were reminded that under the rainbow sign, the Word of God, albeit in a fragmented and distorted form, is already present among the people, for Jesus, according to John, is the 'universal logos' who enlightens every person coming into the world (Jn 1.9). In Chapter 6, we saw that God's Spirit was released in fuller measure to bring additional blessings to the world. Karl Rahner, one of the best advocates within the modern Roman Catholic Church of 'inclusive Christology' argues in the fifth volume of his 20-volume work *Theological Investigations*, that non-Christian religions not only retain elements of a natural knowledge of God but also contain supernatural saving elements of grace.[24] John Wesley was similarly convinced that the Holy Spirit was everywhere at work extending God's prevenient graciousness among all people.[25] Indeed it has been argued from an examination of Wesley's late sermons that he was open to the possibility of eternal life for non-Christians.[26]

Many Western Christians will regard what I have just

written with dismay, for it seems to drain our missionary task of all evangelical content. 'If all are already being saved', the argument runs, 'then what's the point of taking the message of salvation to the nations?' The point is this: people of other faiths and of no faith are not yet experiencing FULL salvation. But here is the rub, neither are we as Western Christians.

We are not experiencing 'full salvation' because our understanding of conversion has been severely distorted by our imperialistic history. Only through a rich encounter and dialogue with others, different from ourselves, will we begin to appreciate and experience the 'fullness of Christ'. Further, we in the rich churches of Britain and North America are not experiencing 'full salvation' because we are trapped in a culture of mammon. As yet individualism, disconnectedness and consumerism has not significantly ensnared the fast growing churches of the Third World, but this destructive triad poses a real health hazard. Only as we embrace new companions and maintain solidarity with the poor will we be liberated from our captivity. As Michael Rodrigo said, 'it is the poor who will ultimately liberate the rich'. Finally, we along with Christians throughout the world are not experiencing 'full salvation' because this is something which belongs to the future. God may indeed liberate, renew and give us a foretaste of his kingdom, but the day of redemption, when righteousness and justice-love are fully established on the earth has not yet dawned. The earth and its ecosystem is still subject to decay; humankind continues to sin and ravage the earth; violence and terrorism paralyse our cities. We have to acknowledge that Christianity has failed to restore righteousness and give adequate incentive for the preservation of the planet. Until the cosmos itself is free, God is not free. And is not the liberation of God the climax of this mission partnership?

What mission is

There have been many attempts over the last seventy years to define mission. The formula describing mission as 'witness' (*martyria*) through 'fellowship' (*koinonia*), 'service' (*diakonia*) and 'proclamation' (*kerygma*) has been the subject of endless discussion. One encounters it in almost every book on the theology of mission after 1952. Its limitations are now generally recognized.[27] My provisional definition in Chapter 1 suggests that mission is some actual or desired movement from one condition to another. It has to do with crossing frontiers.[28] We now see that it is also about transformation, of ourselves, of others and of the world. I now offer my own definition of the mission of the Church:

> Mission is the affirmation, recognition and the planting of communities which witness through their speech, lifestyle and worship to the grace of the Lord Jesus Christ, the inclusive love of God and the fellowship of the Holy Spirit. These communities are 'called out' to work in partnership with the triune God and with others, in the task of preserving, liberating and renewing the earth and all its inhabitants.

The 'great commission' is a mandate commanding us to journey across boundaries because our understanding and experience of the salvation of God is partial and incomplete. We are called to affirm those traditional churches which in some modest way witness to the triune God. Through mutual-discipling we seek to enhance that witness. Sadly some traditional churches may prove to be impervious to the renewing Spirit and will die. On our journey we will stumble across groups of people in unexpected places who are committed to liberation and renewal. They may be embryos waiting to be transformed by the Spirit into ecclesial communities.[29] The 'great commission' further directs us to plant ecclesial communities in places where a gathered church does not exist. This mission of witness and mutual-discipling is uniquely

Christian because it is pursued openly in the power and presence of the triune God.

Thirty years ago Karl Rahner, looking at events in Latin America, Africa, Asia and parts of the United States, prophesied that the future Church would exist largely in the form of scattered base communities mostly among the poor. Local people, through free initiative and association, would in the power of the Spirit seek to engage with the issues of their place.

Rahner's vision of ecclesial communities is similar to John Wesley's. Wesley referred to his churches as 'companies of believers'[30] who act as the 'salt of the earth' or as 'lights of the world'. In fact Wesley operated with two models of Church.[31] One was the historical institution served by professionals like himself. This institution, represented locally in ecclesiastical buildings, was largely out of touch with the new industrial populations. Wesley's principal model was a dynamic 'fellowship of believers' who shared the apostolic experience of God's living presence. It produced its own extraordinary messengers, structures and modes of worship, all in tune with the cultural life out of which the converts came. Wesley established these ecclesial communities on the edge of the Established Church as, what I would describe as, 'parallel' or 'convergent' congregations. His expectation was that they would not only serve to renew the failing mainline institution but also bring happiness and holiness to the world. Sadly the two models could not be held together despite Wesley's efforts, the second later atrophying into the first. Methodism appears to have come full circle!

The actual size of these communities of faith is not without significance. Because we are to be cities set on a hill and lights of the world (Matt. 5.14) community size has to relate primarily to the context and the vocational task required. Sometimes, as in the Subaseth Gedara community, only a small non-threatening group can witness to the way of righteousness. Anything pretentious would be contextually disastrous. In another situation, a larger group may be appropriate if some political aspect of justice or renewal is to be pursued. Yet there are dangers. Competing churches in some contexts aid their own demise.[32] Powerful churches can themselves unwittingly become instruments of oppression. When churches of middle-class people become numerically successful, they lose their capacity to hear the cries of those at the margins. If ecclesial communities are to retain their essential 'saltiness' they will probably always need to be comparatively small, modelling themselves on the vulnerable Jesus.

Although the mission of the Church is to plant itself in every place, its actual presence, because of the elective tides of the Spirit, can be both partial and diverse, permanent or temporary. There should be no attempt to establish a world-wide Christendom. Such a rainbow dream would suffer the same fate as the European Christendom of former centuries. Instead, as a response to the challenge of globalization, the Christian faith must renegotiate its understanding of catholicity. Robert Schreiter mentions three aspects of this new catholicity: the acceptance of the idea of 'commensurability of culture', that is, that Christianity will not be homogeneous; second, an awareness of the fragmented and partial experience of cultures; third, churches will focus on 'the boundaries between those who profit from and enjoy the fruits of the globalization process and those who are excluded and oppressed by it'.[33]

The diverse tapestry of world-wide ecclesial communities will reflect the rich colours and patterns of the Trinity in whom the many are one and the one many. So churches will not replicate themselves like some multi-national McDonald's. There will be a multiplicity of models of the Church. The institution can no longer be regarded as the primary model.[34] Each church will be different so as to represent some aspect of the multiplicity of languages, peoples and cultures. Their unity will not be the product of ecclesiastical joinery but of the Spirit who baptizes with fire and generates diversity. Each local church, as in the New Testament, will be light in structure, ever ready to respond to its own moment of *kairos*. Partnership links between different ecclesial communities through prayer, shared learning, mutual exchange of members and itinerant ministry, will save them from parochialism and demonstrate catholicity. Thus ecclesial communities will ebb and flow to the tides of the Spirit. God is not creating a new set of ecclesiastical institutions but rather a 'fluid' Church reflecting the dancing life of the Trinity, in whom unity and diversity make music together.

The death of the Church in Britain

People tell me I have a romanticized view of Third World Christianity and a rather negative one of Western Christianity. Certainly my knowledge and experience of the World Church is very limited. This is not true of my dealings with the Church in Britain. That I remain within it, and do so joyfully for most of the time, surely testifies to my belief that God has not abandoned the Church. Many individual churches, however, have a limited lifespan because they have marginalized themselves and live in a 'far country' of the congregation's childhood memories. They have not connected up with the post-modern culture of contemporary British society which regards them as being 'highly institutionalized, patriarchal and bourgeois in character'.[35] Like the younger son in the 'far country' (Lk. 15.16), such churches have lost contact with the Father and live on a spiritual starvation diet. They have almost forgotten the rich feast of music and dancing which celebrates the return of the lost and the coming alive of the dead (v. 32).

Callum Brown charts the inevitable decline of Christian Britain and rightly pours scorn on the facile responses of church leaders who naively think they can reverse the process through changing the ecclesiastical structure or the liturgy and optimistically predict an upturn which does not happen and will not happen.[36] The cultural changes which have taken place are of such magnitude that the Church in its present form will only continue 'to exist in some skeletal form'.[37]

Before 1800 Christian piety had been located in 'evangelical masculinity', after 1800 in femininity. The 1960s signalled the 'ungendering' of British Christianity which has resulted in a religious vacuum. The search for faith is now conducted outside traditional Christian institutions and is driven by ideas of personal development and consumer choice.[38] John Drane in his *McDonaldization of the Church* latches onto 'consumer choice' when he examines some of the so-called 'growing' churches in Britain. What is really happening, he says, is that dissatisfied Christians from the dead churches are either leaving or 'shopping-around' for a more lively church. Membership growth in one church precipitates a fall of membership in another in an overall saga of decline.[39] Kenneth Leech remarks that, in a narcissistic culture like ours, 'spirituality is in danger of becoming an essentially private pursuit'.[40]

Some see hope in the ecumenical dream, believing that renewal will come when the traditional mainline churches accept each other and pool their resources. These mammoth institutions sadly drag their weary feet forward when they should be galloping ahead to avoid their own extinction. Little progress can be made, according to Alister McGrath, because ecumenism has 'become the last refuge of the theological bore'.[41] The ecumenical agenda cannot work, he says, because a liberal agenda is irrelevant in today's world of growing conservative evangelical churches.

Since the late eighties a new interest in spiritual realities has swept through Western culture. It has tragically by-passed the churches.[42] John Drane passes a devastating indictment on the institutional Church when he says, 'we seem to have ended up with a secular Church in a spiritual society'.[43] Michael Riddell similarly concludes that 'the greatest barrier to the gospel in contemporary Western culture is the Church'.[44] Locked in an iron cage and controlled by an ecclesiastical elite of clergy and powerful lay persons, the Church in Britain has become a stagnant pool.[45] How can fresh streams of spiritual life flow again into the institutional Church in Britain?

John Finney provides us with an important clue for the

re-evangelization of Britain. His book *Recovering the Past* contrasts the Roman and the Celtic styles of mission. The Roman pattern was to 'set up a skeleton organization and then evangelize. The Celtic pattern was to gather the people and then set up an appropriate framework for them.'[46] The Celtic bishops were not bureaucrats but evangelists who worked at the fringes. The monks, who were mainly lay persons, were *peregrinati* (wanderers) who like Abraham of old prayed and went.[47] Theirs was a Trinitarian and charismatic faith of wonder and miracle.[48] Worship was not in church buildings but centred on the high crosses dotted about the countryside.

The resurrection of the Church in Britain

We have seen that when churches free themselves from ecclesiastical mumbo-jumbo and move their centres to the edge, the breath of the Spirit is able to blow the cobwebs away. Like the apostle Peter, in Acts 10, comfortable dwellers in the mainline churches of Britain are being called to forsake the familiar and enter the uncomfortable world of God's extramural activities. In the house of Cornelius the outsider, the reluctant Peter experiences a new Pentecost. Henceforth Christianity will flourish not in the homelands of Judaism, but in the Gentile world.

The Pentecostal wind is blowing strongly. The future of Christianity no longer lies with the traditional mainline churches but with many forms of Pentecostalism and Evangelicalism. Already on the world stage, Pentecostalism is the most significant alternative to Roman Catholicism, having shunted the traditional Protestant groupings to the sidelines.[49] In Europe and the United States, the Pentecostal and the new Evangelical churches not only nibble away at the edges of the mainline churches but draw out many of its younger clientele. Pentecostalism grows because, unlike the mainline liberal churches, it affirms the traditional evangelical faith and makes real demands of its members.[50] It uses language, music and oral forms of communication which relate to the poor and the marginalized.[51] Its members not only express high levels of commitment but have a real passion for the gospel.

Philip Jenkins suggests that along with the Pentecostalists, the Roman Catholic Church can survive and thrive, which we would expect given its emphasis on inculturation and solidarity with the poor. However, says Jenkins, it will do so only in as far as it adopts the conservative tone of African and Latin American Catholicism rather than the liberal and 'relativistic theories' of Roman Catholics in the Northern hemisphere.[52] It would seem that the future lies with the theologically conservative.

Vibrant and conservative expressions of Christianity are not without their blind spots, as some worried theologians from the traditional churches are all too ready to point out. It is not all sour grapes for what they fear, in a world of violence, is the explosive cocktail of enthusiasm and fundamentalism, and rightly so. It has been said that 'a fundamentalist is simply an evangelical who is angry about something'.[53] Fanaticism and terrorism are spawned by conviction and anger. While conviction fuels the rapid numerical growth of Christianity it also generates energy in other faiths and ideologies. McGrath says, 'Fundamentalism is essentially a "reactive" movement which emerges in response to the perception of a threat to the core values of a people or group.'[54] One can immediately see why crusading ventures of any kind from the supposedly Christian West serve only to inflame fundamentalist expressions of other faiths in different parts of the world. What drives fundamentalism is fear of Western secularism which in turn generates reactions which swell the ranks of the fundamentalists.

Because, in Britain, secularism has deeply penetrated the life and being of the traditional mainline churches, many of their members will be suspicious of churches which, according to their perception, have absorbed fundamentalism. If the traditional churches and the fast growing churches are to escape their respective temptations of despair or hubris, then there must be creative dialogue between them. This is what ecumenical discussion should really be about.

Since the sixties, 'church bashing' has been a popular pastime, the assumption being that the Church as an institution is finished. Like the seven churches in the opening chapters of the biblical book of Revelation, the credibility of the Church is being called into question. But God has not left himself without witnesses. Some measure of restoration and renewal can be achieved through repentance and change. John Henry Newman was surely right to point out that 'if the Church is to remain the same, it must change'.

Church growth theory propounds three necessary forms of church corresponding to size: the cell (3–12 people), the congregation (25–175 people) and the celebration (175+ people).[55] Traditional mainline Protestant churches have focused on the 'congregation', even when size has been below or above the numbers suggested. Because of the problems enumerated above, I suspect that in the next few decades this Sunday congregational model, so beloved of the traditional churches, will move to midweek locations or wither still further. The working model for the future will be regular meetings of the cell and occasional large gatherings for consultation and celebration. Cells can develop into full ecclesial communities. In the Malaysian context, as we have seen, they expand rapidly. In the Saccidananda Ashram and even more so in Subaseth Gedara, the ecclesial community remains small, but no less influential. In Britain such cells may form ecclesial communities within the traditional ecclesiastical institutions or they may, as was the case with Methodism in the eighteenth century, develop alongside as 'societies' or 'classes'.[56] One young Methodist theologian sees the future of Christianity in term of a 'complex network of networks' rather than as large-scale institutions.[57]

What are the marks of ecclesial communities which signal the resurrection of the Church in Britain? Many of their characteristics have already been described in Chapters 3, 5 and 7. There will be burning faith and conviction, a real passion for the gospel and a desire to share it. They will be churches with a vision, where people, seeing beyond themselves, catch glimpses of a new world. They will be communities of belonging, where relationships and not rules set the agenda. They will be places of embrace, where a special welcome will be given to the poor, the marginalized and those ostracized by society. In such communities people will learn how to respect others, work for justice caring for the earth and all its creatures. Real demands will be expected of their members who will pray, study the Scriptures and disciple each other as they seek 'to obey all that Jesus commanded'. They will be places which encourage imagination, inculturation, exploration and risk-taking. They will often be counter-cultural communities.

These ecclesial communities will not necessarily be located in traditional church buildings. There must, however, be a physical space in which people can either be still or move, laugh or cry, sing and dance. While the liturgy and life in these communities will be related and expressed through cultural forms which resonate with the new worshippers, they will also draw from the rich treasures of Christian theology, tradition, hymnology and liturgy. There will be few books apart from the Bible. Few pews will be found or ecclesiastical furniture which clutter the space. But there must be a holy place with imaginative symbols to set it apart and evoke wonder and mystery. The times, days and dates of gatherings will not be set in stone. There will be minimal structure, no clerical domination and no control from outside, though there must be ministerial oversight. Above all, these ecclesial communities will reflect a spirituality of grace and gratitude. They are to be gatherings in which people, hungry for spiritual reality, are fed. Here the Eucharist will be celebrated in such a manner that the worshippers will be broken and blessed. A table will be set in the wilderness as well as in the holy place. Such ecclesial communities will be 'rainbow' communities of healing and hope reflecting the pain-love of the triune God.

9

The way of mission: the music and the dancing

The father said to his servants, 'Quick! Bring the best robe and put it on him. Put a ring on his finger and sandals on his feet. Bring the fatted calf and kill it. Let's have a feast and celebrate. For this son of mine was dead and is alive again; he was lost and is found.' So they began to celebrate. Meanwhile, the older son was in the field. When he came near the house, he heard music and dancing. (Lk. 15.22–5)

Music and dancing can be heard in the background as the parable of the lost son reaches its climax. The younger son is inside, but the elder brother is still outside. The father, his joy mingled with sadness, cannot fully rejoice and join in the dance. How can the elder brother be persuaded to come in? How can he come to understand that relationships come before rules and that embrace is better than exclusion? The previous chapter sought to answer the question 'what is mission'? This final chapter addresses the 'how?' of mission.

Christians, empowered by the Holy Spirit are, in the words of our definition, to 'witness through their speech, lifestyle and worship to the grace of the Lord Jesus Christ, the inclusive love of God and the fellowship of the Holy Spirit'. We propose to explore the 'how?' of mission by examining the features of speech and lifestyle, which roughly correspond to 'proclamation' (*kerygma*) and 'service' (*diakonia*). We shall conclude by reflecting on the liberation of the God of covenant, who is both the object and subject of worship.

The way of mission: the music and the dancing

Proclamation and dialogue

On the Sabbath day, the apostle Paul went into the synagogue at Pisidian Antioch and preached to a mainly Jewish congregation (Acts 13.16, 44). He quoted the Scriptures and declared the Word (Acts 13.16).[1] His approach and style of communication could not be more different when, some months later, he addressed the sophisticated Athenians in the open air on the Mars Hill. Instead of referring to the Jewish Scripture he quotes a pagan poet (Acts 17.28). He talks not about what he has read but about what he has seen. His message is not about a Christ who justifies believers, freeing them from slavery to the law of Moses (Acts 13.39), but about 'a man' who frees all people from ignorance. Put simplistically, the message to the Jewish insiders is about salvation, the message to the Greek outsiders is about illumination. More intriguing still is the fact that Paul does not name the name of 'Christ' in speaking of an 'unknown God'. In both contexts there is an inclusive universal appeal which disturbs his hearers. In both cases mention of 'resurrection' sends a ripple of unease through the audience.

Kenneth Cracknell overturns William Ramsay's view that Paul made a bad mistake in changing his missionary approach for Athens. Cracknell quotes Deissmann who regards Acts 17 as 'the greatest missionary document in the New Testament'.[2] In Acts 17, Luke uses the word *dialogein*, 'to argue', 'to dispute' or 'to dialogue'. Rather than abandoning this experimental method, Paul adopts it wholeheartedly during his two-year ministry in Ephesus where he 'dialogues' in the synagogue.[3] When polarization occurs he moves into a lecture hall where he perseveres until the whole of the province 'heard the word of the Lord' (Acts 19.10). Later when Paul is really up against it, dialogue moves from discussion to testimony (Acts 26).

When mission moves from the centre to the edge, the mode of speech changes. Words of communication are not written but oral, statement becomes story, the verbal idea becomes a visual image, declaration becomes exploration, package becomes pilgrimage. Outside the ecclesiastical institution, dialogue and testimony become the principle forms of witness by word. Paul engages in dialogue because God has not left himself without witnesses in the world for, as we saw in Chapter 2, fragments of this Word, which enlightens every person who comes into the world, are scattered across creation. Dialogue is possible because, as Father Michael says, 'the logos is found inside of dia-logue'. The shape, form, language and content of dialogue will vary according to context. Father Michael in a beautiful theological passage describes how dialogue is possible in a Buddhist context of poverty:

We must study within this soil. But there is a wind blowing through creation. This wind shatters all the values which make for greatness. At the heart of everything there is only the air, the sunlight, the soil, the fire, the wave and the lotus. We have to discern the *saradharma*, the depth-values, at the heart of all faiths. Yet you cannot study these unless you are baptized into their context. Then you are able to hear the sound, the *om* – which has yet to find expression in word. But how do we acquire the hearing? We do this by studying the sacred texts until we lose our very selves. We, like the Buddhist, must seek refuge in the *dharma*. We do not take God to people. We do not take Christ to people, for there is only the Word and with the Word there is no wastage. The Word is buried in the soil of the world. We hear the sound of it in the countryside of Galilee; that is the place where the poor live. For the Word is hidden amongst the voiceless, but it can make them vocal and articulate. We have a saying, 'Even if the mouth lies, the tongue cannot.' The sound is there, though the words may be different. And the words are only heard when they come to us from the depths of silent pain.[4]

The rainbow covenant shows that respect for people and their culture is fundamental. Since God calls us into a mission partnership with himself we seek, through dialogue, to establish partnerships with others. God's Spirit has always been at work amongst the nations, for 'in him we all live and move and have our being' (Acts 17.28). Michael Rodrigo shows himself to be a faithful disciple of the Vatican II *Lumen Gentium* document when he states that life, goodness and truth, wherever found, should be regarded as springing from God.[5] In advocating a 'dialogue with life', he is urging us to follow in the steps of St Paul who sought to tease out the substance of belief in 'the unknown God'. Since the embrace of the Father reaches out into the 'far country', God's Spirit will already be at work before we get there.

In May 1966 Vincent J. Donovan, a Roman Catholic priest based at the Loliondo Mission in East Africa, wrote to his bishop deploring the total failure of their efforts to evangelize the Masai. He requested permission to leave his existing job of running the mission station and simply go as he was, to talk with the Masai about Jesus Christ. His book, *Christianity Rediscovered*, describes his subsequent journey from the centre to the edge, and recounts excerpts of his conversations with these so-called unreachable people. There is an illuminating moment in one of these encounters. He is asked by a Masai villager, 'Has your tribe found the High God? Have you known him?' Donovan was about to give an affirmative reply when something made him pause and reflect on the 'Almighty God' of the Western Church; the God Hitler addressed in his speeches, the God invoked by an American cardinal to bless the 'soldiers of Christ' in Vietnam:

> I finally spoke out again, and I marvelled at how small my voice sounded. I said something I had no intention of saying when I had come to speak to the Masai that morning: 'No, we have not found the High God. My tribe has not known him. For us, too, he is the unknown God. But we are searching for him. I have come a long, long distance to invite you to search for him with us. Let us search for him together. Maybe, together, we will find him.'[6]

God wishes, through the process of dialogue and mutual discipling, to enable us and the people we meet to grow towards full salvation. They, like us, have limited understanding. Through dialogue with new partners we both begin to see what we have not seen before:

> Meeting people across boundaries in the plurality of our post-modern world is not a matter of delivering our truth but of allowing their incompleteness to begin to fill up our own and our incompleteness to fill up theirs so that together we not only critique and challenge each other but also enlarge and complement one another until the whole can become greater and more resourceful than our separate parts.[7]

Both parties are changed. This is illustrated in Peter's encounter with Cornelius. The Italian centurion is told by an angel to send men to Joppa and 'bring one Simon who is called Peter' (Acts 10.5). The apostle comes; preaches to the assembled company; the Holy Spirit falls upon them and Cornelius and his household are converted. But Peter is also changed. Ironically, this is a much more difficult matter. God in a dream invites him to eat unclean animals. He refuses. Three men from Cornelius arrive with a message. He is perplexed. The Spirit prompts him. He delays. Intransigence marks his every step. Yet finally he grasps a new truth. 'Truly I perceive that God shows no partiality, but in every nation anyone who fears him and does what is right is acceptable to him' (Acts 10.34). Conversion to Christ takes place, when in a process of mutual encounter through dialogue, the Holy Spirit changes both parties. Cornelius is converted and joins the Church. Peter is converted to a new vision of how to live under the rainbow sign.

The contemporary spirit

John Drane says that 'the Church simply cannot expect to continue to survive for long into the twenty-first century in its present form'.[8] Doing more of the same, simply precipitates its decline. In Britain we have a secularized Church in a society hungry for spiritual reality.

Mary Grey gives us two cameos of this quest for 'spirit'. The first is the decree by the Blair Government that there should be a stately dome in Greenwich to celebrate the third millennium. But what was to be contained in these caverns, and above all, what was to be placed in the Spirit Zone? Was this primal womb-like structure a sign of the death of creativity and religious zeal or was it a sign of a vast spiritual vacuum waiting to be filled? [9] Mary Grey's other example is not institutionally driven from the top but it springs up from the earth. She speaks of flowers in places connected with accidents, informal shrines to help us remember, doves released into the air and a rediscovery of the sacredness of life. This upsurge of the Spirit in ordinary people is in stark contrast to the vacuousness of the traditional institutional Church.[10] She suggests that spirit-life in the new millennium can no longer be divorced from the physical realities of our natural world. This spirit-life will not be delivered from the top by secularized institutions but will arise from the bottom.

If we are to dialogue about spiritual realities then, like Vincent Donovan in East Africa, some suitably gifted ministers and lay-persons must move to the edge of the ecclesiastical institution and identify with people touched by the spirit of the rainbow covenant.

John Drane gives a pertinent illustration of this in his reflections on the 'Dunblane Massacre'.[11] As he approached the gate of the school in which the killings had taken place, he saw a gang of youths who took from their pockets sixteen night lights – one for each of the children who had been shot. They placed them in a circle, lit them, and then wondered what to do next. Spotting John Drane, who they identified as a minister, they called him and said, 'You'll know what to say'. With tears rolling down his face, he had no idea what to say or how to say it. His brief prayer, however, triggered something in the group:

One said, 'What kind of world is this?' Another asked 'Is there any hope?' Someone said, 'I wish I could trust God.' 'I'll need to change.' said a fourth one. As he did so, he looked first at me, and then glanced over his shoulder to the police who were on duty. He reached into his pocket and I could see he had a knife. He knelt again by the ring of candles, and quietly said, 'I'll not be needing this now', as he tucked it away under some of the flowers lying nearby.

They were, reflects John Drane, expressing 'repentance' though the word would be unfamiliar to them. They were reaching out for spiritual reality. Neither John Drane nor these lads were ready for proclamation or testimony. Yet this was holy ground, for the Holy Spirit was surfacing producing a moment of *kairos* and offering the possibility of dialogue. From such a soil as this, the shoots of new ecclesial communities spring up.

But there are now darker things going on. One of the effects of secularization has been the deregulation of institutional religion. This has not led to religions assuming a lesser role, but rather the opposite. As pluralism eats away at the identity of communities, religious symbols and traditions are used to legitimize the demonic behaviour and exclusive actions of groups.[12]

In his *Reflections on the 11th September and Its Aftermath*, Rowan Williams tells us how living realities are turned into symbols, and that symbolic values are used to imprison reality.[13] The World Trade Center and the Pentagon are symbols of American economic and military dominance, but in their destruction hundreds of ordinary people of uncertain civic status died. Some were Muslims. This symbolic outrage populated the world with more symbols so that Muslims are now regarded as 'potential terrorists', Sikhs are abused and asylum seekers distrusted. We now 'use people to think with'.[14] Our responses become simplified as we verbally strike out using the language of crusade and war; beguiled by the fantasy that high-tech assault weapons do not touch civilians and that wars can be fought without our own soldiers being killed. Jonathan Sacks somberly comments:

> The tensions that September 11 exposed have not diminished. The Middle East is at boiling point. Europe has been simmering with religious and ethnic conflict. There has been violence in India, Pakistan, Kashmir. It would be hard to identify any factor that has made prospects for peace anywhere brighter now than they were a year ago. Is there a key to conflict resolution? Is there anything that has power to generate hope in regions of despair? Can we ever turn enemies into friends?[15]

In the Sri Lankan world of terrorist violence, Father Michael saw that dialogue had to be more radical; deepening into a dialogue with life itself so that toxic religious elements are exposed, symbols investigated and fantasies confronted. In today's polarized and violent world, each of us has become a victim and an oppressor, indeed it has been persuasively argued by René Girard that religion itself produces surrogate victims.[16] Justice and peace cannot be pursued without religious dialogue nor should religious dialogue be separated from a political commitment to the task of liberating the earth and all its inhabitants.

Two essentials

Two essential factors must shape the 'how' of mission. They are encapsulated in the terms 'inculturation' and 'solidarity with the poor'. We are given illustrations of what these words mean in our encounters with Bede Griffiths and Michael Rodrigo. If the First World Church is to grow numerically, organically, conceptually and incarnationally (see Chapter 7) our witness in speech, lifestyle and worship must embrace these two missiological elements.

McGavran argues that the culture of growing churches must relate to the culture of the wider community from which the members come. We have already spoken of 'inculturation' as a necessary missiological process whereby the symbols and mores of the outside community are appropriated, not un-critically, by the Christian community (Chapter 3).[17] The Saccidananda Ashram of Father Bede illustrates this. If the growing centre of a church is the edge then the church must let go of many of the things it holds dear. This lesson has been heeded by some in North America. The Willow Creek Mega-Churches seek to create a Church free from ecclesiastical red tape. Their initiators, Bill Hybels and Dave Holmbo, recog-nized that in most Western churches, outsiders have to fight their way through 'a jungle of obsolete Christian cultural trappings to find out about Jesus'.[18] With the removal of most of the traditional baggage and by using contemporary Western forms of expression, these 'seeker-sensitive churches' have reconnected themselves to the aspirations and cultural life of the people they are trying to attract.

There is, however, a flip side to this. While growing churches embrace their cultural context they are also required, if they are to retain their integrity, to be 'counter-cultural communities'. Christian disciples must question the cultural norms of the community from which they come. An ecclesial community is a 'called out' community where members, through baptism, are invited to establish solidarity with the poor, the vulnerable and the marginalized. The Subaseth Gedara community is a good example of this. Aloysius Pieris takes this further when he says that baptism is not simply a negative protest, nor a demonstration of passive solidarity with the poor, but is a calculated strategy against mammon.[19] Metropolitan Geevaghese Mar Osthathios argues that eccle-sial communities must become 'kenotic communities' living simply so that the poor may simply live, 'for the rich will never part with power unless they are forced to'.[20] Kenneth Leech tells us how the record of the British churches on matters of race, sex and class is a denial of the fundamental understand-ing of baptism as a sign of liberation.[21]

In Chapter 4 I argued that God elects people not because

they are deserving but because 'they hurt'. Michael Taylor, one-time director of Christian Aid, says that God puts the poor first because they have not heard good news for a long time.[22] Marginalized, powerless and broken people are better able to hear the good news of a vulnerable God; indeed in the ministry of Jesus 'the poor heard him gladly'. The global growth of the Church of the poor testifies to this. The poor are sceptical of anything good coming from the rich. The poor, according to Michael Rodrigo, are the true transmitters of the Jesus event.[23] They are chosen to bring good news to us, to open the eyes of the blind! There can be no 'full-salvation' for the First World Church if we are not in solidarity with the poor. Wesley believed the poor could teach us about freedom, joy, sharing, faith and community.[24] The marginalized can liberate us from our captivity to mammon.[25] Theodore Jennings gives a stinging indictment of Methodist churches which forget this:

Methodism was conceived as a call to scriptural holiness. Holiness means the imitation of the divine love which comes to us without worldly power and influence to dwell with us in a radical solidarity and sacrificial generosity. Without this love for the least, all our 'church growth' strategies lead to apostasy. Without the holiness of solidarity with the poor and despised all our evangelization will only produce conversions to religious paganism. Unless we offer a radical alternative to the middle-class life style we will be but a religious reflection of the world that is perishing. No. Methodism will not cease to exist. But unless we look beyond mere symptoms of what Wesley diagnosed as the underlying malady we will be only building larger and fancier sepulchers for a 'dead sect, having the form of religion but without the power'.[26]

Speech, lifestyle and discipleship

The theological basis of our understanding of mission is the mystery of God as revealed in the Trinity. There are three entry points into this triune mystery of which one is the particularity of Christ. Because the rainbow covenant is our theological starting point, there is much to be said in our contemporary post-modern context for beginning where Paul began in Athens – with a dialogue about the 'unknown God' and a conversation about the way in which his Spirit uses symbols to touch our lives.

Insight can be gained through dialogue but we cannot produce it of ourselves. According to the New Testament, we see through the illumination of the Holy Spirit. 'Unless one is born anew he cannot see the kingdom of God . . . unless one is born of water and the spirit he cannot enter the kingdom of God' (Jn 3.3f.). Moments of revelation are *kairos* events within time and history (2 Cor. 6.1–2). We cannot force a revelation, we can only pray and wait for the tides of the Spirit. Illumination, however, does not necessarily lead to any measurable change in lifestyle. People can become fruitless hearers of the Word rather than doers of it (Matt. 7.21–7). This, as we have seen, is a real problem for Christians in the enlightened West who prefer to turn revelation into words rather than into action. Some theologians, while acknowledging that our human reason is subject to all manner of ills because we are sinners, still think that 'truth' can be turned into a series of theological statements.[27] In our encounter with God we are, instead, like Jacob at Peniel (Gen. 32.22) who found himself wrestling with Someone who blesses but slips effortlessly from his grasp. As T. F. Torrance says, 'the truth of God because it is both human and divine comes in the form of mystery. It tells us that behind the objectivity disclosed there is an infinite depth of reality.'[28] Abstract statements of divine truth are 'dead'. They can be spoken, explored, rewritten, handed down from the past, but they will only 'live' within us and become our own through obedience and the power of the Holy Spirit.[29]

The living witness required of us is the fruit of a personal experience of the grace of God. John Wesley before 1738 obediently dragged himself and others along a disciplined and discipling ascetic way[30] until that *kairos* moment when he received the assurance of faith through the power of the Holy Spirit. Then his lifestyle was marked by the joyful witness of a son who had returned from the 'far country' and not the reasoned faith of one who had slaved in his own backyard.

Passion, conviction and lifestyle are essential ingredients of witness; but do we necessarily have to invite people to 'name the name' of Christ in order to experience the salvation of God (Rom. 10.9)? Many titles have been given to Jesus as Christians have attempted to articulate their understanding of him. Jesus, however, 'does not hand out a ready-made christology on a plate'.[31] Christological titles are the by-product of distinct missionary encounters with the non-Christian world. Many of these titles lose their significance as soon as they are transferred across a cultural barrier. For example the title *messiah* becomes anachronistic and meaningless in a total Greek/ Roman environment. No single name or expression can sum up the identity of Jesus, not even the phrase 'son of man', used over sixty times in the Synoptic Gospels.[32] Names fall away from him like leaves from the autumn trees. He cannot adequately be described within the contingencies of history:

> To say, 'Jesus is the Word' is not enough; the word must be heard and executed for one to be saved. To say 'Jesus is the path' is not enough; one must walk the path to reach the end. Moreover, not all who obey the Word nor all who walk the path are obliged to know its proper name to be Jesus. For, what saves is not the 'name' of Jesus in the Hellenistic sense of the term 'name', but the name of Jesus in the Hebrew sense of 'the reality' that was seen to be operative in Jesus, independent of the name or designation we may attach to it. In fact, the knowledge of the name or title is not expected by the eschatological Judge, but knowledge of the path is expected (Matt. 25.37–9, 44–6).[33]

Persons, I observe, who are primarily concerned with names and titles are often the very people who seek to have power 'over'; for 'naming' is a method of controlling. We may honour God with the lips but our hearts may be far from him (Mk 7.6). A theological word game can be played which detracts from the cost of self-denying discipleship. When faced with such theological controllers, Jesus has no option but to confront their false naming of him (Jn 8.58).[34]

Within the kingdom those who play the 'naming game' will themselves be judged by the titles they use, for 'not everyone who says to me, Lord, Lord, shall enter the kingdom of heaven' (Matt. 7.21). Jesus takes the negative way (*via negativa*) of the hidden God (*Deus Absconditus*) and refuses to accept oral confession as the only condition for experiencing salvation (Mk 10.18). Instead, would-be disciples touched by the grace of God must follow in his footsteps and so discover what full salvation means. Jesus is simply reiterating the old mandates given to Abraham and to all who, in subsequent generations, put their faith in the promises of God. Thus the hidden way is the dangerous yet joyful way of the cross (Heb. 12.2).

On 4 November 1987, 12 armed men in uniform surrounded Michael Rodrigo's home and accused him of hiding a member of the JVP (Janata Vimukthi Peramuna) who had supposedly shot and injured a local businessman. The next day the armed men again returned and told him not to admit members of the JVP to the community. Father Michael retorted that he could not distinguish JVP members from others and refused to exclude anyone. He was not interested, he said, in party politics but only in poor people. In the days which followed, the situation was so tense that the small community debated whether they should at least abandon Subaseth Gedara for a time. Michael said:

> We are a part of the people and they must be consulted. I have consulted them and they are unanimous that we should stay. Otherwise they would have no one to turn to in

their difficulties. For me the voice of the people is the voice of God. They have decided we should not leave them and that is the voice of God for me. In any case I will not foist my opinion on anyone. If the community decides otherwise, I will abide by it. After all my bones are light enough to be carried away.[35]

On the evening of 10 November, Father Michael himself prepared the altar for Mass. It was a small table about six inches above ground level. It was a table set in the wilderness as a sign of the blessing and brokenness of the new covenant. It was a sign of hope in a context of violence. He told members of the community that Mass was to be at the earlier hour of five o'clock so that 'we will have plenty of time for the Lord and we have to make a decision today'. During Mass Father Michael recited Psalm 130, 'Out of the depths have I called unto you O Lord'. Afterwards he said:

> The lasting things are love and relationship with the people. These things will last even in eternity. Don't be afraid. We will commit ourselves to God. Into your hands, O Lord, I commit my spirit.[36]

At about 7.30 p.m. as he was saying the blessing with the sisters, at the end of the Mass, Michael Rodrigo was shot through the head by an unknown assassin. He died instantly. There was so much blood it poured out from under the door. Blood was also found in the chalice they had used for communion. His skull was shattered in pieces but the Buddhist villagers later gathered up his brain and eyes, and buried them in the herb garden, saying 'These are the eyes which saw our condition and this is the brain that guided us.'[37]

There is little doubt in my mind that he was killed because of his commitment to the abandoned poor, which in many parts of Sri Lanka was held to be subversive activity. I am told he had a premonition that something was going to happen and had deliberately stayed on at Subaseth Gedara. Now he is gone and the poor have lost a father.

Like the whisper on the wind, the sound of Father Michael's melodious voice came to me when I heard of his violent death:

> Were I the oil
> And you the living flame, Lord
> We'll burn together unto death
> For death is Life.
> Drowned in my teeming incapacities
> Thy Hand sustains me.
> The breath of Life, Thy Spirit
> Keeps me, flickering
> For weak and faltering be my will
> The gush-wind that enlivens without extinguishing
> My flame.[38]

Worship and the dance of God

In Chapter 1 I spoke of Thomas Merton and of his Sri Lankan visit to Polonnaruwa. We have come full circle, back to Sri Lanka and my own personal moment of revelation at Subaseth Gedara. In this final section of my book I therefore return to Merton who says, 'What is serious to men is often very trivial in the sight of God. What in God might appear to us as "play" is perhaps what He Himself takes most seriously.'[39] I now see the death of Father Michael from the perspective of what Merton called 'the dance of God':

> The Lord plays and diverts Himself in the garden of his creation, and if we could let go of our own obsession with what we think is the meaning of it all, we might be able to . . . follow Him in His mysterious, cosmic dance. We do not have to go very far . . . to catch the echoes of that dancing.

> Like the elder brother (Lk. 15.25), we can hear the music and the dancing. The real question is will we join in?

> For the world and time are the dance of the Lord in emptiness . . . and no despair of ours can alter the reality of things,

or stain the joy of the cosmic dance which is always there. Indeed, we are in the midst of it, and it is in the midst of us, for it beats in our very blood, whether we want it to or not.[40]

The Cappadocian Fathers of the fourth century coined the term *perichoresis* (*circumincession*) to describe the relatedness of persons within the Trinity. The word literally means 'to proceed about each other'. It is a sort of dance of reciprocal identification suggesting movement and flux within God; a finding and loosing; a sort of successive interaction of two persons 'in the sustaining presence of the Other', a third all-enveloping ambiance. Both the younger and elder sons will join with the father in the music and dancing. God's covenant partners are likewise swept up by the music, 'intertwining without entirely interlocking'.[41] There is a circling and spiral-ling of partners in joy and pain until both are transfigured in each other, lost in a love-making out of which new universes are conceived and born. Through his partnership with us the triune God recreates a world in which violence, fragmenta-tion, separation and individualism are overcome and commu-nal, symbiotic solidarity is realized. Worship celebrates this.

The new ecclesial communities will welcome 'music and the dancing' for they express grace and gratitude in the Spirit. Worship of the Trinity must be expressed through movement in space. Writing in 1978 about worship, J. G. Davies spoke of 'dance' as an all-important feature of worship. 'In dance we discover what we as physical beings can and will do . . . Dancing itself is not an amusing distraction . . . it is an explo-ration, a voyage of discovery.'[42] This is a dance in which pews are swept away and the resurrection of the body celebrated.[43] It is part of much inculturated worship in the 'far country' of Africa. In dance we swirl within the Trinity.

This Trinity is not self-contained but an 'open-Trinity',[44] always ready to embrace new covenant partners. Ecclesial communities will reflect this. Christians, unlike the Jews, are not a third race defined with hard boundaries, for in a violent world divided by tribalism God does not seek to create yet another tribe.[45] Instead, God's people open up spaces within themselves so that other partners can participate in the dance of creation. When our hands and hearts are open in gracious embrace, then our souls and bodies become the music of love.

> None is an outsider, all are insiders, all belong. There are no aliens, all belong in the one family, God's family, the human family.[46]

As a Methodist I stand within the tradition of Wesley's optimism of grace. I am reminded that his own confident hope in the Spirit's renewing work increased with the years, so that towards the end of his long life he was able to say:

> He [God] is already renewing the face of the earth. And we have strong reason to hope that the work he hath begun he will carry on unto the day of his Lord Jesus; that he will never intermit this blessed work of his Spirit until he hath fulfilled all his promises; until he hath put a period to sin and misery, and infirmity, and death; and re-established universal holiness and happiness, and caused all the inhabitants of the earth to sing together, 'Hallelujah! The Lord God omnipotent reigneth!' 'Blessing, and glory, and wisdom, and honour, and power, and might be unto our God for ever and ever!' [47]

The liberation of God

Each covenant is impregnated with hope. So too is the 'great commission'. That is why our obedience and partnership is joyful. Moltmann in his *Theology of Hope* says that the sin of despair is the sin of not taking the covenant promise of God seriously and therefore not doing justice but wallowing in resignation, inertia and melancholy.[48] We are on a journey of joy anticipating the transformation of all things.

The Eastern Church uses the Greek word *theosis* to describe the end of our existence.[49] The vision is of a transfigured universe 'filled with all the fullness of God' (Eph. 3.19). This majestic conception of 'divinization' (*theosis*), found in the great religions of the East, has been preserved in the liturgy of the Orthodox and Syrian churches who remain unimpressed by our Western obsession for projects and proselytizing.[50] The light of grace shines in the liturgy and like a magnet draws out those who dwell in the 'far country'.[51] I was made aware of this during my stay with the Mar Thoma Church in Kerala. For them, worship is both the means and the end of mission. *Theosis* anticipates the re-tuning of a discordant creation by repairing the twin pillars of righteousness and justice. *Theosis* is the rainbow blessing which re-establishes unbroken solidarity in and between individuals, communities, peoples, nations, animals, plants and biosphere.

Theosis touches the whole created order making it impossible to conceive of any group of people who might be rebellious to the end. The last Word has to be God's not humankind's. God excludes no one. The concluding verses of Paul's great exposition of election in Romans speak of the final homecoming of all people. God's limitless grace will overcome even the most obdurate opposition for 'God has consigned all men to disobedience that he may have mercy upon all' (Rom. 11.32). God's grace is at work through history and beyond history, gathering all things together in Christ and admitting no defeat (Eph. 1.5–10). There will no longer be a 'far country' (Lk. 15.13) in which the rebellious can hide. The loving Father now inhabits the 'far country' so that even those 'far off' are near.

God's grace has no limiting clauses or finite boundaries. In the covenants God limited himself in time and space to work with us, but at the end of history when time is transcended this activity of God becomes unconfined. God is free to reveal himself as God beyond covenant because we, his covenant partners through the perfecting processes of sanctification, are able at last to rejoice in the dancing freedom of the 'children of God' (Rom. 8.21–2). Happiness is ultimately inevitable:

The perfection of God and the consummation of the world are two aspects of the same reality. God achieves perfection only through the world, and the world attains its consummation only in God. Both are works of the Spirit, which is co-generated by God and the world. Spirit is the wind that draws and drives the world toward its goal, and Spirit is the refining fire which purifies without consuming. God becomes a whole in which otherness is not reduced to the same, even in the eternal divine history. This history is the history of love in freedom. Our vocation is to be a small part of it.[52]

When the divine nature has become imprinted on our hearts (2 Pet. 1.4) God will dwell in us and we in God. That will be the moment of God's liberation when he is free to be all in all (1 Cor. 15.28). This is the end and purpose of mission. However, it is not the end of the end, for even though the concealed God (*Deus Absconditus*) becomes the revealed God (*Deus Revelatus*), there is no diminishing of the hiddenness. The mystery remains; indeed with every further revelation the mystery deepens. Perfection is not static, it remains an ongoing journey of growth and exploration into the ever increasing possibilities of infinite love.[53]

In mission God coerces no one yet surrenders to no one. He calls all into a partnership with himself to attain the glorious liberty of the children of God. This God of covenant delights in freedom; his own freedom, freedom for every human being on this planet and freedom for the whole created order. In the end every 'no' is swallowed up in a glorious 'yes'. The salvation of God unexpectedly springs up in our faces. Others will be changed; but change will also take place in us as we discover God to be more wonderful than we had ever dared to imagine. For the present, however, the God of mission beckons us on, for the work is incomplete. Nelson Mandela's words, which end his autobiography *Long Walk to Freedom*, are also a description of all who journey in the 'far country':

I have walked that long road to freedom. I have tried not to falter; I have made missteps along the way. But I have discovered the secret that after climbing a great hill, one only finds that there are many more hills to climb. I have taken a moment here to rest, to steal a view of the glorious vista that surrounds me, to look back on the distance I have come. But I can rest only for a moment, for with freedom come responsibilities, and I dare not linger, for my long walk is not yet ended.[54]

Epilogue

John Wesley was born on 17 June 1703. The Southampton Methodist Synod has celebrated the tercentenary of this event by committing itself to a mission initiative entitled Our Providential Way. During the year I have visited the 25 circuits seeking to challenge the 270 churches to 'have a go' at planting new 'parallel' or 'convergent' congregations. We seek, much as Wesley did, to focus not on the centre but on the edges of the institutional Church. The vision of Our Providential Way can only be realized by working with others in a network of partnerships across the District and beyond. We seek ecumenical partners, local statutory or voluntary partners in the community and, where appropriate, partnerships with churches overseas. The priorities of Our Providential Way are:

To focus on evangelism.
To give weight to work which focuses on outreach and work with younger people.
To put resources into specified areas of work where Christians are seeking to stand alongside the weak and disadvantaged.
To give priority in term of the deployment of personnel and resources to circuits and churches where people are demonstrating an imaginative desire to build on the past and step out in faith.

This book sets out the theological basis for Our Providential Way. The questions in the Appendix attempt to anchor missionary initiatives in reflective theology. The Christian

Epilogue

Church, as Bishop Crispian Hollis reminded us at the beginning, has the responsibility of bringing 'the Good News into all strata of humanity, and through its influence transforming humanity from within and making it new'.

Prayer

Father of love,
    We thank you that your rainbow covenant
        embraces all people and lures them to fullness of life.
Jesus redeemer,
    We thank you that your new covenant
        brings blessing in brokenness and creates gratitude
            through grace.
Spirit of God,
    We thank you that you dance through creation
        scattering sparks of hope and weaving networks of
            community.
May we, as your covenant partners,
    work with you in healing the wounds and scars
        of our violent world.
                Amen

Appendix: questions for discussion

Chapter 1: What is mission? Into the far country

1. Write your own definition of mission. (Keep a copy of what you have written. You will need it in a later session.)
2. What experience have you had of being in a 'far country'? How has it affected you?
3. In your church, how do you strike a proper balance between Bible, tradition, reason and experience?

Chapter 2: The rainbow covenant

1. How do you respond to the suggestion that God's saving grace is at work in every nation and people? Can you illustrate this in some way?
2. How is your church demonstrating an ecological concern for the planet?
3. Does God really want all other 'faiths' or 'religions' to grow?

Chapter 3: From exclusion to embrace

1. Can you give examples of how Western culture has affected (a) what your church does, (b) how you personally understand Christianity?
2. When you think about the present state of the world, what grounds for optimism exist?
3. How do you explain the presence of evil and the recurrent cycles of violence?

Appendix: questions for discussion

Chapter 4: A particular covenant

1. How do you understand the theological idea of 'election'?
2. Does this chapter throw any light on the conflict between Israel and the Palestinians?
3. How should Christians relate to (a) Jews, (b) members of another faith or religion?

Chapter 5: From centre to edge

1. Tell a personal story of how you have received insight from some marginalized or disadvantaged group of people.
2. Reflect on some recent situation of conflict, disagreement or violence between Christians and others. What was actually going on?
3. Many churches are self-absorbed. How do you propose changing this?

Chapter 6: A covenant in the Spirit

1. Describe your own personal experience of the Holy Spirit.
2. How does your church live by the Holy Spirit?
3. When did your church last experience a moment of *kairos*? What happened?

Chapter 7: From decline to growth

1. Give your church a health check using the four criteria of Orlando Costas.
2. What 'church growth' insights might be important for your church?
3. What are you doing to demonstrate solidarity with the poor and marginalized?

Chapter 8: What is mission? Coming to the Father

1. Compare your definition of mission (Session 1) with the

one suggested in this chapter. What do you understand the purpose of mission to be?

2. Would it be possible to set up a partnership or 'twinning' scheme between your church and a church overseas (or in some other 'far country')?

3. What will the Church of the future look like?

Chapter 9: The way of mission: the music and the dancing

1. What methods of evangelization are being used in your church?

2. To what extent has your level of commitment changed or deepened as a result of this study?

3. What have you learnt about the God of mission?

Notes

Foreword

1. Pope Paul VI, *Evangelii Nuntiandi*, Boston: Pauline Books and Media, 2002, para. 18.
2. Jn 3.8.
3. Lk. 15.22.
4. Pope Paul VI, *Evangelii Nuntiandi*, para. 41.

Prologue

1. Tom Stuckey, *Rainbow, Journey and Feast: Biblical Covenants and a Theology of Mission*, Delhi: ISPCK, 1988.
2. Tom Stuckey, *Understanding New Testament Letters Today*, Jigsaw Series, London: Bible Society, 1985; and *Understanding Old Testament Prophets Today*, Jigsaw Series, London: Bible Society, 1985. Also articles and reports on the charismatic movement, healing and wholeness, mission and evangelism, urban council estates, growing churches, mission in Matthew's Gospel, mission alongside the poor, the future of theological formation and leadership in the Church.
3. Gordon Wakefield, *Methodist Spirituality*, Peterborough: Epworth Press, 1999, pp. 3f., and Theodore Runyon, *The New Creation: John Wesley's Theology Today*, Nashville: Abingdon Press, 1998, pp. 212f.

1. What is mission? Into the far country

1. M. Thomas Thangaraj, *The Common Task: A Theology of Christian Mission*, Nashville: Abingdon Press, 1999, p. 27.
2. See Moravian Spirituality, in Gordon Wakefield (ed.), *A Dictionary of Christian Spirituality*, London: SCM Press, 1983, p. 269.
3. Geoffrey Moorhouse, *The Missionaries*, London: Eyre Methuen, 1973, pp. 37–41.

4. D. W. Bebbington, *Evangelicalism in Modern Britain*, London: Unwin Hyman, 1988, pp. 38f.; also Henry Rack, *Reasonable Enthusiast: John Wesley and the Rise of Methodism*, London: Epworth Press, 1989, pp. 114f.

5. Skevington Wood, *The Inextinguishable Blaze*, London: Paternoster Press, 1960, pp. 107f.

6. *Selections from the Journals of the Revd. John Wesley*, London: C. H. Kelly, 1891, p. 95. Theodore Jennings Jr, 'Good News to the Poor in the Wesleyan Heritage', in James Logan (ed.), *Theology and Evangelism in the Wesleyan Heritage*, Nashville: Kingswood Books, 1994, pp. 139f.

7. *Hymns and Psalms*, London: Methodist Publishing House, 1983, No. 264.

8. N. Allen Birtwhistle, 'Methodist Mission', in R. Davies, R. George and G. Rupp (eds), *A History of the Methodist Church in Great Britain*, Vol. 3, London: Epworth Press, 1983, p. 43.

9. Helmut Thielicke, *The Waiting Father: Sermons on the Parables of Jesus*, London: James Clarke & Co., 1966.

10. Raymond Fung, *The Isaiah Agenda*, Risk Book Series, Geneva: WCC, 1995.

11. Bede Griffiths, *The Cosmic Revelation*, Bangalore: Asian Trading Corporation, 1985.

12. See 4 December 1968, in P. Hart and J. Montaldo (eds), *The Intimate Merton*, A Lion Book, Oxford: Lion, 2000, p. 435. See also Monica Furlong, *Merton: A Biography*, London: Darton, Longman & Todd, 1985.

13. Thangaraj, *Common Task*, p. 22.

14. Lawrence James, *The Rise and Fall of the British Empire*, London: Abacus, 2000, p. 21.

15. James, *Rise*, pp. 22f.

16. J. Verkyl, *Contemporary Missiology*, Grand Rapids: Eerdmans, 1978, p. 3.

17. Thangaraj, *Common Task*, p. 38.

18. Lesslie Newbigin's important book on mission *The Open Secret*, Grand Rapids: Eerdmans, 1981, is shaped by this 'Trinitarian Faith'.

19. Gil Bailie, *Violence Unveiled: Humanity at the Crossroads*, New York: Crossroad, 1997.

20. Paul Tillich, *Systematic Theology*, Vol. I, London: Nisbet, 1953, p. 18.

21. William J. Abraham, 'The Revitalization of United Methodist Doctrine and the Renewal of Evangelism', in Logan, *Theology and Evangelism*, pp. 41ff.

22. Thomas A. Langford, *Methodist Theology*, Peterborough: Epworth Press, 1998, p. 6.

23. Thangaraj, *Common Task*, p. 40.

24. Colin W. Williams, *John Wesley's Theology Today*, London: Epworth Press, 1962, pp. 32f.

25. Don Browning, *A Fundamental Practical Theology*, Philadelphia: Fortress Press, 1991.

26. John Munsey Turner, *John Wesley: The Evangelical Revival and the Rise of Methodism in England*, Peterborough: Epworth Press, 2002.

2. The rainbow covenant

1. Miroslav Volf, *Exclusion and Embrace: A Theological Exploration of Identity, Otherness, and Reconciliation*, Nashville: Abingdon Press, 1996, pp. 156f.

2. Karl Barth, *Church Dogmatics*, IV.1, Edinburgh: T&T Clark, 1961, p. 22.

3. Karl Barth, *Church Dogmatics*, II.2, Edinburgh: T&T Clark, 1957, p. 566.

4. Karl Barth, *Church Dogmatics*, III.2, Edinburgh: T&T Clark, 1960, pp. 203f.

5. Frances Young and Kenneth Wilson, *Focus on God*, London: Epworth Press, 1986, p. 84.

6. Barth, *Dogmatics*, IV.1, p. 25.

7. Jürgen Moltmann, *The Trinity and the Kingdom of God*, London: SCM Press, 1981, pp. 10f.

8. Barth, *Dogmatics*, IV.1, pp. 187f.

9. Volf, *Exclusion*, pp. 157f.

10. Volf, *Exclusion*, p. 156.

11. John Robinson has argued in his book *Truth Is Two-Eyed*, London: SCM Press, 1979, pp. 14f., that there can be two opposite and apparently incompatible explanations and both are necessary.

12. Richard Henry Drummond, *Towards a New Age in Christian Theology*, Maryknoll, NY: Orbis Books, 1985, p. 6.

13. Barth, *Dogmatics*, IV.1, p. 27.

14. Wesley Ariarajah, *The Bible and People of Other Faiths*, Risk Book Series, Geneva: WCC, 1985, pp. 6f.

15. Drummond, *Towards*, pp. 10f.

16. G. Von Rad, *Wisdom in Israel*, London: SCM Press, 1978, p. 10.

17. Stuart Blanch, *The Christian Militant*, London: SPCK, 1978, p. 28.

18. Kenneth Cracknell, *Towards a New Relationship*, London: Epworth Press, 1986, p. 50.

19. A. B. Come, *An Introduction to Barth's Dogmatics for Preachers*, London: SCM Press, 1963, pp. 162f.

20. T. F. Torrance, *Karl Barth: An Introduction to His Early Theology 1910–1931*, London: SCM Press, 1962, p. 55f.
21. Karl Barth, *Church Dogmatics*, IV.3a, Edinburgh: T&T Clark 1961, p. 86.
22. Barth, *Dogmatics*, IV.3a, pp. 97f.
23. Eberhard Busch, *Karl Barth*, London: SCM Press, 1976, p. 410.
24. Barth, *Dogmatics*, IV.3a, pp. 454f.
25. Barth, *Dogmatics*, IV.3a, p. 453.
26. Barth, *Dogmatics*, IV.3a, p. 432.
27. Barth, *Dogmatics*, IV.3a, p. 429.
28. Barth, *Dogmatics*, IV.1, p. 27.
29. Thangaraj, *Common Task*, p. 124.
30. Thangaraj, *Common Task*, p. 127.
31. Anne Primavesi, *From Apocalypse to Genesis*, Burns & Oates Ltd, 1991, pp. 205f.
32. Ian Bradley, *God Is Green*, London: Darton, Longman & Todd, 1990, p. 93.
33. Matthew Fox, *Original Blessing*, New Mexico: Bear & Co., 1983, p. 184.
34. Fritjof Capra, *The Turning Point*, London: Wildwood House, 1982, pp. 33f.
35. Johannes Seoka, 'African Culture and Christian Spirituality', in Mogezi Guma and Leslie Mitton (eds), *An African Challenge to the Church in the 21st Century*, Cape Town: Salty Print, 1997, pp. 2f. and 12f.
36. Bede Griffiths, *The Marriage of East and West*, London: Collins, Fount Paperbacks, 1983, pp. 156f.
37. Bradley, *God Is Green*, pp. 1f.
38. Kosuke Koyama, *Three Mile an Hour God*, London: SCM Press, 1979, p. 5.
39. John Drane, *The McDonaldization of the Church*, London: Darton, Longman & Todd, 2001.
40. Kenneth Clark, *Civilization*, London: BBC and John Murray, 1969, pp. 276f.
41. Runyon, *New Creation*, pp. 202f.
42. Victor P. Hamilton, *The Book of Genesis, Chapters 1–17*, Grand Rapids: Eerdmans, 1990, p. 313.
43. Karl Barth, *Church Dogmatics*, III.4, Edinburgh: T&T Clark 1961, p. 312.
44. Raymond Panikkar, 'The Category of Growth in Comparative Religion: A Critical Self-Examination', in *Harvard Theological Review* 66, 1973, p. 135.
45. Peter Heslam, *Globalization: Unravelling the New Capitalism*,

Cambridge: Grove Books Ltd, 2002, pp. 18f.

46. Barth, *Dogmatics*, III.4, p. 344.

47. Runyon, *New Creation*, pp. 204f.

48. David Landes, *The Wealth and Poverty of the Nations*, London: Little, Brown & Co., 1998, p. 516.

49. Harvey T. Hoekstra, 'Preparatory Materials for the Fifth Assembly of the WCC', in *Evangelism in Eclipse*, Exeter: Paternoster Press, 1979, p. 229.

50. The original meaning of the verb 'to save', *yasha* (from which we get the names of Joshua and Jesus) means 'to give space'.

51. Leonard Hulley, Louise Kretzschmar and Luke Lungile Pato (eds), *Archbishop Tutu: Prophetic Witness in South Africa*, Cape Town: Human and Rousseau, 1996 p. 138.

52. S. Samkange and T. Samkange, *Hunmuism or Ubuntuism*, Salisbury Zimbabwe: Graham Books, 1980, p. 55.

53. Samkange and Samkange, *Hunmuism*, p. 51.

54. Samkange and Samkange, *Hunmuism*, p. 39.

55. Hulley, Kretzschmar and Pato, *Archbishop Tutu*, p. 137.

56. Hulley, Kretzschmar and Pato, *Archbishop Tutu*, p. 102.

57. Hulley, Kretzschmar and Pato, *Archbishop Tutu*, p. 79.

58. Antjie Krog, *Country of My Skull*, London: Jonathan Cape, 1999, pp. 109f. Also Tinyiko Maluleke, 'Truth, National Unity and Reconciliation in South Africa', in Guma and Mitton, *African Challenge*, pp. 109f.

59. *Babylon Talmud, Shabbath 31a* (private conversation with Michael Rodrigo).

60. *Ibn Madja, Introduction 9* (Rodrigo).

61. *Anushana Pavrva 113.7* (Rodrigo).

62. *Sutt Nipata, No. 149* (Rodrigo).

63. John V. Taylor, *The Primal Vision*, London: SCM Press, 1963, p. 10.

3. From exclusion to embrace

1. Griffiths, *Marriage*, p. 8.

2. Michael Gallagher, *Clashing Symbols: An Introduction to Faith and Culture*, London: DLT, 1997, pp. 36f.

3. Gallagher, *Clashing*, p. 47.

4. Vinay Samuel, 'Gospel and Culture', in Vinay Samuel and Albrecht Hauser (eds), . *Proclaiming Christ in Christ's Way: Studies in Integral Evangelism*, Oxford: Regnam Books, 1989, pp. 70f.

5. Pope Paul VI, *Evangelii Nuntiandi*, 20.

6. J. Scherer and S. Bevens, *New Directions in Mission and*

Evangelization 1: Basic Statements 1974–1991, Maryknoll, NY: Orbis Books, 1992, pp. 44–5.

7. Scherer and Bevens, *New Directions*, p. 120.

8. Scherer and Bevens, *New Directions*, p. 140.

9. Kathryn Spink, *A Sense of the Sacred*, London: SPCK 1988, p. 115.

10. Spink, *Sense*, p. 172.

11. Gallagher, *Clashing*, p. 66.

12. Jyoti Sahi, *Stepping Stones*, Bangalore: Asian Trading Corporation, 1986.

13. Bede Griffiths, *Return to the Centre*, Collins: Fount Paperbacks, 1984, p. 41.

14. Israel Selvanayagam, 'Crossing Over and Coming Back', in Martin Forward (ed.), *A Great Commission: Christian Hope and Religious Diversity*, New York: Peter Lang, 2000, p. 276.

15. Diana Eck, 'The Perspective of Pluralism in Theological Education', in S. Amirtham and S. Wesley Ariarajah (eds), *Ministerial Formation in a Multi-Faith Milieu*, Geneva: WCC, 1986, p. 67.

16. Emmanuel Jacob, 'Discipleship and Mission: A Perspective on the Gospel of Matthew', *International Review of Mission*, XCI (360) (January 2002), p. 106.

17. Benedict T. Viviano, 'The Gospel according to Matthew', *The New Jerome Biblical Commentary*, London: Geoffrey Chapman, 2000, p. 632.

18. John Ziesler, 'Matthew and the Presence of Jesus (part 1)', *Epworth Review*, 11 (1) (January 1984), p. 58.

19. Griffiths, *Marriage*, p. 10.

20. *Redemption Hymnal*, Elim Publishing House, 1967, No. 746.

21. Carl F. Hallencreutz, 'Tambaram Revisited', *International Review of Mission*, LXXIII (289) (January 1984).

22. *Hymns and Psalms*, London: Methodist Publishing House, 1983, No. 238.

23. Harvey Cox, *The Secular City*, London: SCM Press, 1965, p. 1.

24. Callum Brown, *The Death of Christian Britain*, London and New York: Routledge, 2001, p. 193.

25. Brown, *Death*, p. 198.

26. Hoekstra, *Evangelism in Eclipse*.

27. Alister McGrath, *The Future of Christianity*, Oxford: Blackwell Publishers, 2002, pp. 2f.

28. Part of a letter sent by the conference to invited churches encouraging them to pray. Found in Orlando Costas, *Christ outside the Gate*, Maryknoll, NY: Orbis Books, 1984, p. 139.

29. Alasdair MacIntyre, *After Virtue: A Study in Moral Theory*,

London: Duckworth, 1981, p. 245.

30. Alasdair MacIntyre, *Three Rival Versions of Moral Enquiry: Encyclopaedia, Genealogy, and Tradition*, Indiana: University of Notre Dame, 1990, p. 8.

31. Nicholas Lash, *Theology on the Way to Emmaus*, London: SCM Press, 1986, p. 201.

32. Jonathan Sacks, *The Dignity of Difference: How to Avoid the Clash of Civilizations*, revd edn, New York: Continuum Publishing, 2003, pp. 24f.

33. Peter Heslam, *Globalization: Unravelling the New Capitalism*, Cambridge: Grove Books, 2002.

34. Heslam, *Globalization*, p. 13.

35. D. Bosch, *Believing in the Future: Towards a Missiology of Western Culture*, Valley Forge: Trinity Press International 1995, pp. 47f.

36. Rowan Williams, *Writing in the Dust: Reflections on 11th September and Its Aftermath*, London: Hodder & Stoughton, 2002, pp. 59f.

37. Langdon Gilkey, *Message and Existence*, London: SCM Press, 1979, p. 155.

38. Barth, *Dogmatics*, IV.1, pp. 187f.

39. C. S. Song, *Third-Eye Theology*, Guildford and London: Lutterworth Press, 1980, p. 70.

40. Albert Camus, *The Rebel*, tr. Anthony Bower, London: Vintage Books, 1956, p. 297.

41. John Roth, 'A Theology of Protest', in Stephen Davis (ed.), *Encountering Evil*, Edinburgh: T&T Clark, 1981, p. 11.

42. John Polkinghorne, *Science and Christian Belief: Theological Reflections of a Bottom-Up Thinker*, London: SPCK, 1994, p. 81.

43. Ian Bradley, *The Power of Sacrifice*, London: DLT, 1995, p. 66.

44. Bradley, *Power*, p. 71.

45. Eugene Peterson, *Under the Unpredictable Plant*, Grand Rapids: Eerdmans, 1992, pp. 163f.

46. Jürgen Moltmann, *Theology and Joy*, London: SCM Press, 1973, pp. 40f.

47. Nigel Calder, *Violent Universe*, London: BBC, 1969.

48. W. Brueggemann, 'Covenanting as Human Vocation', *Interpretation*, XXXIII (2) (April 1979), pp. 122–23

49. Critique by David Griffin, in Davis, *Encountering*, p. 27.

50. Song, *Third-Eye*, p. 70.

51. Barth, *Dogmatics*, IV.1, p. 222.

52. Barth, *Dogmatics*, IV.1, p. 185.

53. Quoted by Song, *Third-Eye*, p. 61.

54. Bradley, *Power*, p. 74.

55. Quoted by Jürgen Moltmann, *The Future of Creation*, London: SCM Press, 1979, p. 65.

56. C. E. Rolt, 'The World's Redemption', quoted by Moltmann, *Trinity*, p. 34.

4. A particular covenant

1. Barth, *Dogmatics*, II.2, p. 10.

2. Emil Brunner, *The Christian Doctrine of God: Dogmatics*, Vol. 1, London: Lutterworth Press, 1964, p. 31.

3. Barth, *Dogmatics*, II.2, p. 105.

4. Barth, *Dogmatics*, II.2, pp. 29f.

5. John Calvin, *Institutes of the Christian Religion*, The Library of Christian Classics, Vol. XX, London: SCM Press, 1961, pp. 920f.

6. Barth, *Dogmatics*, II.2, pp. 511f.

7. Barth, *Dogmatics*, II.2, p. 233.

8. C. S. Song, *The Compassionate God*, London: SCM Press, 1982, p. 22.

9. G. Von Rad, *Genesis*, London: SCM Press, 1961, p. 149.

10. Jonathan Sacks, *The Dignity of Difference: How to Avoid the Clash of Civilizations*, revd edn, New York: Continuum Publishing, 2003, p. 55.

11. Jonathan Sacks, *The Dignity of Difference: How to Avoid the Clash of Civilizations*, New York: Continuum Publishing, 2002, p. 53.

12. J. Verkuyl, *Contemporary Missiology*, Grand Rapids: Eerdmans, 1978, p. 92.

13. C. S. Song, 'From Israel to Asia – a Theological Leap', in G. Anderson and T. Stransky (eds), *Mission Trends, No. 3*, Toronto: Paulist Press; Grand Rapids: Eerdmans, 1979, p. 216.

14. Lesslie Newbigin, *The Gospel in a Pluralist Society*, London: SPCK, 1989, pp. 86f.

15. Bengt Sundkler, *The World of Mission*, London: Lutterworth Press, 1965, p. 14. Peter Cotterell, in *Mission and Meaninglessness*, London: SPCK, 1990, pp. 54f., approaches this in a similar way focusing, as most evangelicals do, on the exclusive passages of . Scripture and making Jn 14.6. the interpretive centre for his theological understanding of mission. The particularity of Christ need not be placed in this restricting straitjacket.

16. Sundkler, *World*, p. 25.

17. Verkuyl, *Contemporary*, p. 301.

18. Song, *Compassionate*, p. 69.

19. Walter Brueggemann, *Texts That Linger, Words That Explode*, Minneapolis: Fortress Press, 2000, p. 97.

20. Brueggemann, *Texts*, p. 96.

21. Von Rad, *Genesis*, p. 183. Also Hamilton, *Genesis*, p. 431.

22. E. Speiser, *Genesis: Introduction, Translation and Notes*, New York: Doubleday, 1964, p. 113: the reference to 'oven'.

23. Takatso Mofokeng, 'Land Is Our Mother: A Black Theology of Land', in Guma and Mitton, *African Challenge*, pp. 42f.

24. Hamilton, *Genesis*, pp. 469f.

25. Hamilton, *Genesis*, p. 473.

26. Hamilton, *Genesis*, pp. 481f.

27. Walter Brueggemann, 'Covenanting as Human Vocation', *Interpretation*, XXXIII (2) (April 1979), p. 119.

28. Brueggemann, 'Covenanting', p. 120.

29. Thangaraj, *Common Task*, p. 128.

30. Walter Brueggemann, 'The Kerygma of the Deuteronomistic Historian', *Interpretation*, XXII (4) (October 1968), p. 390.

31. Thangaraj, *Common Task*, pp. 129f.

32. D. Senior and C. Stuhlmueller, *The Biblical Foundations for Mission*, London: SCM Press, 1983, p. 85.

33. J. Gordon McConville, 'The Old Testament and the Enjoyment of Wealth', in C. Bartholomew and T. Moritz (eds), *Christ and Consumerism*, Carlisle: Paternoster Press, 2000, p. 46.

34. Walter Brueggemann, *The Covenanted Self*, Minneapolis: Fortress Press,1999, pp. 99f.

35. Brueggemann, *Covenanted Self*, p. 101.

36. Brueggemann, *Covenanted Self*, p. 104.

37. Senior and Stuhlmueller, *Biblical Foundations*, p. 86.

38. Walter Brueggemann, 'The "Uncared For" now cared for (Jer. 30.12–17): A Methodological Consideration', *Journal of Biblical Literature*, 104 (3) (1985), p. 420.

39. Brueggemann, *Texts*, pp. 67f.

40. Walter Brueggemann, *Old Testament Theology: Essays on Structure, Theme, and Text*, Minneapolis: Fortress Press, 1992, p. 20.

41. Brueggemann, *Old Testament Theology*, p. 27.

42. Franz Rosenzweig, quoted by Moltmann, *Trinity*, p. 92.

43. Senior and Stuhlmueller, *Biblical Foundations*, p. 87.

44. David Bosch, *Witness to the World: The Christian Mission in Theological Perspective*, London: Marshall Morgan & Scott, 1980, p. 52.

45. Barth, *Dogmatics*, II.2, pp. 206f.

46. David Bosch, *Transforming Mission: Paradigm shifts in theology of mission*, Maryknoll NY: Orbis Books, 1998, p. 62.

47. Barth, *Dogmatics*, IV.1, p. 166.

48. Barth, *Dogmatics*, IV.1, p. 175.

49. J. S. Whale, *Victor and Victim*, Cambridge: Cambridge University Press, 1960, p. 91.

50. F. Hahn, *Mission in the New Testament*, London: SCM Press, 1965, p. 109.

51. Newbigin, *Gospel*, p. 83.

52. Verkuyl, *Contemporary*, p. 141.

53. Volf, *Exclusion*, p. 39.

54. Orlando Costas, *Christ outside the Gate*, Maryknoll, NY: Orbis Books, 1984, pp. 188f.

55. Costas, *Christ*, p. 192.

56. McGrath, *Future of Christianity*, pp. 68f.

57. Walter Brueggemann, 'Disciplines of Readiness', *Occasional Paper No.1, Theology and Worship Unit Presbyterian Church (USA)*, 1988, p. 17.

58. Peter Hodgson, *Winds of the Spirit*, London: SCM Press, 1994, p. 297.

5. From centre to edge

1. Michael Rodrigo, 'I haunted villages with a Mezenod's zeal', *Tissues of Life and Death*, Colombo: Centre for Society and Religion, 1988, p. 36.

2. Tissa Balasuriya, *Planetary Theology*, London: SCM Press, 1984.

3. Michael Rodrigo, 'The Moral Passover from Selfishness to Selflessness in Christianity and the other Religions in Sri Lanka', *Fr. Mike and His Thought, Logos*, 27 (3) (September 1988), Colombo: Centre for Society and Religion.

4. Commission on Theological Concerns of the Christian Conference of Asia (eds), *Minjung Theology, People as Subjects of History*, Maryknoll, NY: Orbis Books, 1981.

5. Michael Rodrigo, 'Towards a More Intensive Dialogue with Buddhists', *Dialogue*, XII (1–3) (1985), Colombo: Ecumenical Institute for Study and Dialogue, p. 14.

6. Michael Rodrigo, 'Liberation: Praxis', *Liberation Theology, Logos*, 24 (1) (March 1985), Colombo: Centre for Society and Religion, p. 123.

7. Rodrigo, 'Towards a More Intensive Dialogue', p. 8.

8. Michael Rodrigo, 'Buddhism and Christianity: Towards the Human Future', *Dialogue*, XIII and XIV (1986–7), Colombo: Ecumenical Institute for Study and Dialogue, p. 96.

9. Rodrigo, 'Buddhism', p. 99.

10. Rodrigo, *Tissues*, p. 22.

11. Rodrigo, 'Buddhism', p. 107.

12. Rodrigo, *Tissues*, p. 45f.

13. David Bosch, 'The Scope of Mission', *International Review of Mission*, LXXIII (289) (January 1984), p. 25.

14. Timothy Gorringe, *Redeeming Time: Atonement through Education*, London: Darton, Longman & Todd, 1986, p. 15.

15. McGrath, *Future of Christianity*, p. 132.

16. Tom Stuckey, 'Dialogue of Life', in Sr Milburga Fernando (ed.), *Father Mike, the Prophet and Martyr*, Logos Publications, Colombo: Centre for Society and Religion, 1989, p. 74.

17. Rodrigo, 'Towards a More Intensive Dialogue', pp. 8f.

18. Balasuriya, *Planetary*, p. 1.

19. Karl Barth, *Church Dogmatics*, IV.4, Edinburgh: T&T Clark 1969, p. 54.

20. Barth, *Dogmatics*, IV.4, p. 15.

21. Vinay C. Samuel, 'The Mission Implications of Baptism, Eucharist and Ministry', *International Review of Mission*, LXXII (286) (April 1983), p. 208.

22. Rom. 1.16; 3.29; Gal. 3.26–8; Col. 3.11; 1 Pet. 2.9.

23. Rodrigo, 'Liberation: Praxis', p. 120.

24. Aloysius Pieris, *An Asian Theology of Liberation*, Edinburgh: T&T Clark, 1988, pp. 49f.

25. Bosch, *Transforming Mission*, p. 81.

26. M. Joseph and M. Zachariah (eds), *Discipleship as Mission*, Kottayam: A & A Printers Private Ltd, 1984, p. 83.

27. Jacob, 'Discipleship and Mission', p. 106.

28. Francis Anekwe Oborji, 'Poverty in the Mission-Charity Trend – Perspective from Matthew', *International Review of Mission*, XCI (360) (January 2002), p. 92.

29. M. Goulder, *A Tale of Two Missions*, London: SCM Press, 1994; James D. G. Dunn, *Unity and Diversity in the New Testament*, London: SCM Press, 1977.

30. J.G. Davies, *The Early Christian Church*, London: Weidenfeld & Nicolson, 1965, p. 216.

31. Owen Chadwick, *A History of Christianity*, London: Phoenix Illustrated, 1997, pp. 58f.

32. Chadwick, *History*, p. 81.

33. Bosch, *Transforming Mission*, pp. 209–13.

34. Bosch, *Transforming Mission*, pp. 225–26.

35. John De Gruchy, *Reconciliation: Restoring Justice*, SCM Press, 2002, p. 115.

36. K. S. Latourette, *A History of the Expansion of Christianity*, Vol. II, London: Eyre & Spottiswoode, 1939, pp. 16f and 311f.

37. Bamber Gascoigne, *The Christians*, New York: William Morrow & Company Inc., 1977, p. 113.

38. Stephen Neill, *A History of Christian Missions*, Harmondsworth: Penguin Books, 1971, pp. 450–1.

39. Quoted in J. S. Spong, *Why Christianity Must Change or Die*, New York: HarperSanFrancisco, 1998, p. 48.

40. De Gruchy, *Reconciliation*, pp. 116f.

41. John V. Taylor, 'The Theological Basis of Inter-Faith Dialogue', in G. Anderson and T. Stransky (eds), *Mission Trends, No. 5*, Toronto: Paulist Press; Grand Rapids: Eerdmans, 1981, p. 96f.

42. Drummond, *Towards a New Age*, p. 183.

43. José M. Bonino, 'The Present Crisis in Mission', in G. Anderson and T. Stransky (eds), *Mission Trends, No. 1*, Toronto: Paulist Press; Grand Rapids: Eerdmans, 1974, p. 41.

44. Volf, *Exclusion*, p. 61.

45. Philip Jenkins, *The Next Christendom: The Coming of Global Christianity*, Oxford: Oxford University Press, 2002, pp. 163f.

46. Jenkins, *Next Christendom*, p. 13.

47. René Girard, *I See Satan Fall like Lightning*, Leominster: Gracewing, 2001. p. 24.

48. Girard, *I See*, pp. 83–4.

49. Girard, *I See*, pp. 19f.

50. Girard, *I See*, p. 157.

51. Robert Schreiter, *Constructing Local Theologies*, London: SCM Press, 1985, pp. 72f.

52. Donald Messer, *A Conspiracy of Goodness*, Nashville: Abingdon Press, 1992, p. 141.

53. Ian Summerscales, 'Some Implications of Inter-faith Dialogue', *Epworth Review*, 14 (3) (September 1987), p. 80.

54. Bosch, *Witness to the World*, p. 53.

55. Thomas Carlisle, in Verkuyl, *Contemporary Missiology*, p. 100.

56. Rodrigo, 'Liberation: Praxis', p. 128.

57. Rodrigo, 'Towards a More Intensive Dialogue', p. 12.

58. Rabindranath Tagore, *Gitanjali*, London: MacMillan Papermac, 1986, p. 29.

59. Volf, *Exclusion*, p. 38.

60. Volf, *Exclusion*, pp. 50f.

6. A covenant in the Spirit

1. Wolfhart Pannenberg, *Jesus, God and Man*, London: SCM Press, 1968, p. 170.

2. Hodgson, *Winds*, pp. 277f.

3. Cornelius Plantinga, *Not the Way It's Supposed to Be: A Breviary of Sin*, Grand Rapids: Eerdmans, 1995, p. 29.

4. John V. Taylor, *The Go-Between God*, London: SCM Press, 1972, p. 61.

5. Hodgson, *Winds*, p. 279.

6. Taylor, *Go-Between*, p. 49.

7. Mary Grey, *The Wisdom of Fools*, London: SPCK, 1995, p. 128.

8. Taylor, *Go-Between*, p. 3.

9. The actual sentence is slightly different in each reading. The word 'new' is not present in all versions but all refer to 'covenant' (*diathekes*).

10. Trevor Dennis, *Imagining God: Stories from Creation to Heaven*, London: SPCK, 1997, p. 13.

11. Volf, *Exclusion*, p. 154.

12. Jürgen Moltmann, *The Crucified God*, London: SCM Press, 1974, p. 205.

13. J. Denney, *The Death of Christ*, London: Hodder & Stoughton, 1902, p. 166.

14. P. T. Forsyth, *The Justification of God*, London: Hodder & Stoughton, 1906, p. 174.

15. C. E. B. Cranfield, *The Epistle to the Romans*, Vol. 1, ICC, Edinburgh: T&T Clark, 1975, p. 213.

16. K. Kitamore, *The Theology of the Pain of God*, London: SCM Press, 1965, p. 19.

17. De Gruchy, *Reconciliation*, pp. 53f.

18. Claus Westermann, 'Blessing in the Bible and the Life of the Church', in Fox, *Original Blessing*, p. 44.

19. Volf, *Exclusion*, p. 128.

20. Hoo-Jung Lee, 'Experiencing the Spirit in Wesley and Macarius', in Randy Maddox (ed.), *Rethinking Wesley's Theology for Contemporary Methodism*, Nashville, TN: Kingswood Books, 1998, p. 211.

21. J. Jeremias, *The Eucharistic Words of Jesus*, Oxford: Basil Blackwell, 1955, p. 136.

22. Geoffrey Wainwright, *Eucharist and Eschatology*, London: Epworth Press, 1971, p. 58.

23. Gregory Dix, *The Shape of the Liturgy*, Westminster: Dacre Press, 1945, p. 48.

24. O. Culmann and F. J. Leenhardt, *Essays on the Lord's Supper*, London: Lutterworth Press, 1958, p. 16.

25. W. Albright and C. S. Mann, *Matthew: Introduction, Translation and Notes*, New York: Doubleday, 1971, p. 179.

26. C. E. B Cranfield, *The Gospel according to St. Mark*, The Cambridge Greek Testament Commentary, Cambridge: Cambridge University Press, 1955, p. 221.

27. G. D. Kilpatrick, *The Eucharist in Bible and Liturgy*, Cambridge: Cambridge University Press, 1983, p. 361.

28. Tissa Balasuriya, *Eucharist and Human Liberation*, London: SCM Press, 1979, p. xi.

29. Drane, *McDonaldization*, p. 96.

30. Timothy Gorringe, *Love's Sign: Reflections on the Eucharist*, Madurai: Tamilnadu Theological Seminary, 1986, p. 48.

31. Mar Osthathios, *Your Kingdom Come*, Geneva: WCC, 1980, p. 39.

32. Orlando Costas, *The Church and Its Mission: A Shattering Critique from the Third World*, Wheaton, IL: Tyndale House, 1974, pp. 37f.

33. Girard, *I See*, p. 189.

34. Marjorie Suchocki, 'The Perfection of Prayer', in Maddox, *Rethinking Wesley's Theology*, p. 62.

35. Nigel Collinson, *The Land of Unlikeness*, Peterborough: Foundery Press, 1996, p. 56.

36. Brueggemann, *Old Testament Theology*, p. 38.

37. Brueggemann, *Old Testament Theology*, p. 32.

38. Davies, *Early Christian Church*, p. 34.

39. F. F. Bruce, *The Spreading Flame*, Exeter: Paternoster Press, 1958, p. 170.

40. Bruce, *Spreading Flame*, p. 334.

41. Ronald Sider, *Rich Christians in an Age of Hunger*, London: Hodder & Stoughton, 1973, pp. 78f.

42. Sider, *Rich*, p. 95.

43. Hodgson, *Winds*, p. 294.

44. Bosch, *Transforming Mission*, p. 113.

45. Taylor, *Go-Between*, p. 53.

46. Taylor, *Go-Between*, p. 120.

47. Jürgen Moltmann, *The Church in the Power of the Spirit*, London: SCM Press, 1977, p. 86.

48. D. Bonhoeffer, *The Cost of Discipleship*, London: SCM Press, 1959, p. 189.

49. Thomas Merton, *No Man Is an Island*, London: Burns & Oates, 1955, p. 209.

50. José Comblin, *The Meaning of Mission*, Dublin: Gill & Macmillan, 1979, pp. 44f.

51. Quoted by Gordon Rupp, *Principalities and Powers*, London: Wyvern Books, 1965, p. 84.

52. Mortimer Arias, *Announcing the Reign of God: Evangelization and the Subversive Memory of Jesus*, Philadelphia: Fortress Press, 1984, p. 82.

53. Rodrigo, 'Moral Passover', p. 87.

54. Song, *Compassionate*, p. 260.

55. Hoekstra, *Evangelism in Eclipse*, p. 127.

56. Emanuel Sullivan, *Baptised in Hope*, London: SPCK, 1980, p. 47.

57. Sullivan, *Baptised*, p. 47.

58. W. J. Hollenweger, *The Pentecostals*, London: SCM Press, 1972.

59. McGrath, *Future of Christianity*, p. 29.

60. McGrath, *Future of Christianity*, p. 35.

61. Jenkins, *Next Christendom*, 2002, p. 3.

62. Dennis Dutton, 'Wesleyan Evangelism in an Asian Context: A Case Study', in Logan, *Theology and Evangelism*, pp. 127f.

63. 'The difference between receiving the Spirit and being filled with the Spirit, is a difference not of kind, but of degree. In the one case, the light of heaven has reached the dark chamber, disturbing night, but leaving some obscurity and some deep shadows. In the other, that light has filled the whole chamber, and made every corner bright' (William Arthur, 'The Tongue of Fire', quoted in Langford, *Methodist Theology*, p. 67).

7. *From decline to growth*

1. Donald McGavran, *How Churches Grow*, London: World Dominion, 1959, p. 58.

2. McGrath, *Future of Christianity*, p. 66.

3. Michael Riddell, *Threshold of the Future*, London: SPCK 1997, p. 99.

4. Drane, *McDonaldization*, p. 54.

5. Eddie Gibbs, *I Believe in Church Growth*, London: Hodder & Stoughton, 1981, pp. 148f.

6. Roy Pointer, *How Do Churches Grow?*, Basingstoke: Marshalls Paperbacks, 1984, p. 5.

7. Donald McGavran, *The Bridges of God*, London: World Dominion, 1955.

8. James Scherer, 'The Life and Growth of Churches in Mission', in Anderson and Stransky, *Mission Trends, No. 1*, p. 168.

9. Donald McGavran, *Understanding Church Growth*, Grand Rapids: Eerdmans, 1970, p. 26.

10. McGavran, *Understanding*, p. 23.

11. McGavran, *Understanding*, p. 38.

12. McGavran, *How Churches*, p. 16.

13. McGavran, *Understanding*, pp. 223f.

14. Derek Tidball, *An Introduction to the Sociology of the New Testament*, Exeter: Paternoster Press, 1983.

15. McGavran, *Understanding*, p. 242.

16. McGrath, *Future of Christianity*, pp. 47f.

17. Ray Anderson, *Minding God's Business*, Grand Rapids: Eerdmans, 1986, p. 44.

18. C. Peter Wagner, *Church Growth and the Whole Gospel*, San Francisco: Harper & Row, 1981, p. 40.

19. Hans-Ruedi Weber, 'God's Arithmetic', in G. Anderson and T. Stransky (eds), *Mission Trends, No.* 2, Toronto: Paulist Press; Grand Rapids: Eerdmans, 1975, p. 65.

20. Juan Carlos Ortis, *Disciple*, London: Marshall Morgan & Scott, Lakeland, 1975, p. 85.

21. Alan Padgett, *The Mission of the Church in the Methodist Perspective*, Lampeter: Edwin Mellen Press,1992, p. 141.

22. James Gustafson, *The Church as Moral Decision Maker*, Philadelphia: Pilgrim Press, 1970, pp. 122f.

23. Wayne McClintock, 'Sociological Critique of the Homogeneous Unit Principle', *International Review of Mission*, LXXVII (305) (January 1988), pp. 107f.

24. Costas, *Christ*, p. 50.

25. Robin Gill, *Beyond Decline*, London: SCM Press, 1988, p. 80.

26. Costas, *Church and Its Mission*, p. 11.

27. Costas, *Church and Its Mission*, p. 89.

28. Costas, *Church and Its Mission*, p. 90.

29. Costas, *Church and Its Mission*, p. 124.

30. *Selections from the Journals of the Revd. John Wesley*, London: C. H. Kelly, 1891, p. 97.

31. McGavran, *Understanding*, p. 303.

32. *Hymns and Psalms*, London: Methodist Publishing House, 1983, Nos 563, 781, 216, 264, 744.

33. George Hunter III, *The Contagious Congregation: Frontiers in Evangelism and Church Growth*, Nashville: Abingdon Press, 1979.

34. Lesslie Newbigin, *The Gospel in a Pluralist Society*, London: SPCK, 1989, p. 243.

35. George Hunter III, 'The Apostolic Identity of the Church and Wesleyan Christianity', in Logan, *Theology and Evangelism*, p. 160.

36. George Hunter III, *To Spread the Power; Church Growth in the Wesleyan Spirit*, Nashville: Abingdon Press, 1987, p. 41.

37. McGavran, *Understanding*, p. 6.

38. Hunter III, *To Spread*, p. 58.

39. Howard A. Snyder, *The Radical Wesley & Patterns of Church Renewal*, Downers Grove, IL: InterVarsity Press, 1980, pp. 53f.

40. McGavran, *Understanding*, p. 299.

41. McGavran, *Understanding*, p. 307.

42. Costas, *Church and Its Mission*, p. 127.

43. Hunter III, 'Apostolic Identity', p. 159.

44. McGavran, *Understanding*, pp. 245–8.

45. Davies, *Early Christian Church*, p. 34.

46. Tidball, *Introduction*, pp. 93f.

47. Allen Birtwhistle, 'Methodist Missions', in Davies, George and Rupp, *History of the Methodist Church in Great Britain*, Vol. 3, p. 7

48. Jenkins, *Next Christendom*, p. 73.

49. McGavran, *Bridges of God*, p. 225.

50. Newbigin, *Open Secret*, p. 146.

51. Robin Gill, *A Vision for Growth*, London: SPCK, 1994, pp. 56f.

52. Jeremy Paxman, *The English: A Portrait of a People*, London: Penguin Books, 1999, p. 107.

53. Barbara Butler and Tom Butler, *Just Mission*, London: Mowbray, 1993, p. 58.

54. Peter Cotterell, *Mission and Meaninglessness*, London: SPCK, 1990, pp. 158f.

55. Pope Paul VI, *Evangelii Nuntiandi*, 75.

56. McGavran, *Understanding*, p. 281.

57. McGavran, *Understanding*, p. 285.

58. Private conversation.

59. Kenneth L. Carder, 'What Difference Does Knowing Wesley Make', in Maddox, *Rethinking Wesley's Theology*, pp. 29f.

60. Theodore Jennings, 'Good News to the Poor in the Wesleyan Heritage', in Logan, *Theology and Evangelism*, p. 142.

61. Jennings, 'Good News', p. 147.

62. Jennings, 'Good News', p. 153.

63. Theodore Jennings, 'Transcendence, Justice and Mercy', in Maddox, *Rethinking Wesley's Theology*, p. 80.

64. C. Bartholomew and T. Moritz (eds), *Christ and Consumerism*, Carlisle: Paternoster Press, 2000, p. 8.

65. Peter Heslam, *Globalization: Unravelling the New Capitalism*, Cambridge: Grove Books, 2002, p. 11.

66. Harvey Cox, *Fire from Heaven: The Rise of Pentecostal Spirituality and the Reshaping of Religion in the Twenty-First Century*, London: Cassell, 1996, p. 65.

67. Jenkins, *Next Christendom*, p. 2.

68. Senior and Stuhlmueller, *Biblical Foundations*, p. 1.

69. Rosino Gibellini, *The Liberation Theology Debate*, London: SCM Press, 1987, p. 74.

70. James Laney, 'Our New Identity', in Logan, *Theology and Evangelism*, p. 178.

71. Quoted by Mary Grey, *The Outrageous Pursuit of Hope*, London: Darton, Longman & Todd, 2000, p. 78.

8. What is mission? Coming to the Father

1. Bosch, *Witness to the World*, p. 240.
2. Brueggemann, *Old Testament Theology*, p. 35.
3. Brueggemann, *Old Testament Theology*, pp. 30f.
4. Karl Barth, *Church Dogmatics*, II.1, Edinburgh: T&T Clark 1963, p. 184.
5. See Philip S. Watson, *Let God be God*, London: Epworth Press, 1960, p. 95; also Martin Luther, *A Commentary on St. Paul's Epistle to the Galations*, James Clarke & Co., 1961, pp. 43f.
6. Luther, *Commentary*, p. 384.
7. J. Héring, *The First Epistle of St Paul to the Corinthians*, London: Epworth Press, 1964, p. 142.
8. William Stacy Johnson, *The Mystery of God*, Louisville: Westminster John Knox Press, 1997, p. 25.
9. Barth, *Dogmatics*, IV.1, p. 187.
10. Barth, *Dogmatics*, IV.1, p. 192.
11. Volf, *Exclusion*, p. 159.
12. Volf, *Exclusion*, p. 163.
13. Volf, *Exclusion*, p. 164.
14. K. S. Latourette, *A History of the Expansion of Christianity*, Vol. IV, London: Eyre & Spottiswoode, 1947, pp. 44–5.
15. Cotterell, *Mission and Meaninglessness*, pp. 72–5.
16. *The Poisonwood Bible*, London: Faber & Faber, 1999, a novel by Barbara Kingsolver, is an extreme illustration of attitudes which sadly still exist.
17. Moorhouse, *Missionaries*, pp. 226f.
18. Neill, *History of Christian Missions*, p. 313.
19. Allen Birtwhistle, 'Methodist Missions', in Davies, George and Rupp, *History of the Methodist Church in Great Britain*, Vol. 3, pp. 54–6.
20. Thangaraj, *Common Task*, pp. 12f.
21. Paul Younger, *Theology of Vision, Bread, and Politics*, Delhi: ISPCK 1986, pp. 11f.
22. David Hesselgrave, *Communicating Christ Cross-Culturally*, Allahabad: St Paul Publications, 1978.
23. Denton Lotz, 'Peter's Wider Understanding of God's Will', *International Review of Mission*, LXXVII (306) (April 1988), p. 201.
24. Karl Rahner, *Theological Investigations, Volume Five*, London: Darton, Longman & Todd, 1966, pp. 121f.
25. Runyon, *New Creation*, p. 33.
26. Runyon, *New Creation*, p. 35.
27. Bosch, *Transforming Mission*, p. 512.
28. Bosch, *Witness to the World*, p. 17.

29. Thangaraj, *Common*, p. 37.

30. Hunter III, 'Apostolic Identity', pp. 158f.

31. Snyder, *Radical Wesley*, p. 71.

32. Robin Gill, *Competing Convictions*, London: SCM Press, 1989, p. 133.

33. M. Thomas Thangaraj, 'Theological Education in Today's Multi-Religious Setting', in Forward, *Great Commission*, p. 288.

34. Avery Dulles, *Models of the Church: A Critical Assessment of the Church in All Its Aspects*, Dublin: Gill & MacMillan, 1983, p. 187.

35. Tangaraj, *Common*, p. 37.

36. Brown, *The Death*.

37. Brown, *The Death*, p. 198.

38. Brown, *The Death*, p. 196.

39. Drane, *McDonaldization*, p. 39.

40. Kenneth Leech, *The Sky Is Red: Discerning the Signs of the Times*, London: Darton, Longman & Todd, 1997, pp. 121f.

41. McGrath, *Future of Christianity*, p. 85.

42. John Drane, *What Is the New Age Saying to the Church?*, London: Marshall Pickering, 1991.

43. Drane, *McDonaldization*, p. 54.

44. Riddell, *Threshold*, p. 57.

45. Riddell, *Threshold*, p. 13.

46. John Finney, *Recovering the Past*, London: Darton, Longman & Todd, 1996, p. 32.

47. Finney, *Recovering*, p. 56.

48. Finney, *Recovering*, p. 86.

49. McGrath, *Future of Christianity*, pp. 106–14.

50. McGrath, *Future of Christianity*, p. 42.

51. McGrath, *Future of Christianity*, p. 108.

52. Jenkins, *Next Christendom*, pp. 194f.

53. George Marsden, quoted in Leech, *The Sky*, p. 84.

54. McGrath, *Future of Christianity*, p. 75.

55. Pointer, *How Do Churches Grow?*, p. 51.

56. Rack, *Reasonable Enthusiast*, p. 179.

57. Clive Marsh, *Christianity in a Post-Atheistic Age*, London: SCM Press, 2002, p. 113.

9. The way of mission: the music and the dancing

1. F. F. Bruce, *The Book of the Acts*, London: Marshall Morgan & Scott, 1965, pp. 271f.

2. Cracknell, *Towards a New Relationship*, p. 30.

3. Ariarajah, *Bible and People of Other Faiths*, pp. 44f.

4. Stuckey, 'Dialogue of Life', p. 74.

5. Rodrigo, 'Moral Passover', p. 7.

6. Vincent J. Donovan, *Christianity Rediscovered*, London: SCM Press, 1978, p. 46.

7. Michael Taylor, 'Eat, Drink and Be Merry for Tomorrow We Live', Address to the Methodist Conference at Ipswich, 25 June 2001.

8. Drane, *McDonaldization*, p. 156.

9. Grey, *Outrageous Pursuit*, p. 58.

10. Grey, *Outrageous Pursuit*, p. 71.

11. Described in Riddell, *Threshold*, pp. 30f.

12. Volf, *Exclusion*, p. 283.

13. Williams, *Writing*, p. 68.

14. Williams, *Writing*, p. 67.

15. Sacks, *Dignity of Difference*, p. 175.

16. René Girard, *Things Hidden since the Foundation of the World*, London: Athlone Press, 1987, pp. 138f.

17. Ion Bria (ed.), *Go Forth in Peace: Orthodox Perspectives on Mission*, WCC Mission Series, Geneva: WCC, 1986, p. 81.

18. McGrath, *Future of Christianity*, p. 61.

19. Pieris, *Asian Theology*, p. 49.

20. Geevarghese Mar Osthathios, 'Kenosis and Exaltation of the Son of God, the Disciples, the Church and the World', in Joseph and Zachariah, *Discipleship as Mission*, p. 19.

21. Kenneth Leech, *Struggle in Babylon: Racism in the Cities and Churches of Britain*, London: Sheldon Press, 1988, pp. 186f.

22. Michael Taylor, *Good for the Poor; Christian Ethics and World Development*, London: Mowbray, 1990, p. 19.

23. Michael Rodrigo, 'Bible and the Liberation of the Poor', *Dialogue*, XV (1–3) (1988), Colombo: Ecumenical Institute for Study and Dialogue, pp. 75f.

24. Runyon, *New Creation*, p. 190.

25. Williams, *Christ on Trial*, pp. 61f.

26. Theodore Jennings, 'Good News to the Poor', in Logan, *Theology and Evangelism*, p. 156.

27. Douglas Groothius, *Truth Decay: Defending Christianity against the Challenges of Postmodernism*, Downers Grove, IL: InterVarsity Press, 2000.

28. T. F. Torrance, *Theological Science*, London: Oxford University Press, 1969, pp. 148f.

29. Heinrich Vogel, *Consider Your Calling*, London: Oliver & Boyd, 1962, p. 52f.

30. Runyon, *New Creation*, pp. 44f.

31. R. H. Fuller, *The Foundations of New Testament Christology*,

London: Lutterworth Press, 1965, p. 15.

32. A complete reappraisal of the New Testament 'son of man' tradition has been undertaken by Barnabas Lindars. He concludes that even though the early Church puts its understanding of Jesus in the messianic concepts of the time, the term originally started out as an idiomatic feature of Jesus' speech (*Jesus Son of Man*, London: SPCK, 1983, pp. 188f.)

33. Aloysius Pieris, *Love Meets Wisdom: A Christian Experience of Buddhism*, Maryknoll, NY: Orbis Books, 1988, p. 133.

34. A. E. Harvey, *Jesus on Trial: A Study in the Fourth Gospel*, London: SPCK, 1976, p. 58.

35. *Father Michael Rodrigo: Prophet, Priest and Martyr*, Colombo: Christian Workers Fellowship, 10 November 1989, p. 11.

36. *Father Michael: Prophet, Priest and Martyr*, p. 12.

37. *Father Michael: Prophet, Priest and Martyr*, p. 2; also Joseph Samarakone, 'The Trail Blazer', in Fernando, *Father Mike, the Prophet and Martyr*, p. 92.

38. Rodrigo, *Tissues*, p. 8.

39. Thomas Merton, *New Seeds of Contemplation*, New York: New Directions, 1962, p. 296.

40. Merton, *New Seeds*, p. 297.

41. Michael Mayne, *Learning to Dance*, London: Darton, Longman & Todd, 2001, p. 197.

42. J. G. Davies, *New Perspectives on Worship Today*, London: SCM Press, 1978, p. 20 and 34.

43. Mayne, *Learning*, pp. 204f.

44. Moltmann, *Trinity*, pp. 94f.

45. Volf, *Exclusion*, p. 49.

46. Desmond Tutu, *No Future without Forgiveness*, Johannesburg: Rider Books, 1999, p. 213

47. Runyon, *New Creation*, p. 7.

48. Moltmann, *Theology of Hope*, p. 22.

49. Zacharias Mar Theophilius, 'How Costly Is Discipleship', in Joseph and Zachariah, *Discipleship as Mission*, p. 84.

50. Bosch, *Witness to the World*, p. 186.

51. John Meyendorff, 'The Orthodox Church and Mission: Past and Present Perspectives', in Anderson and Stransky, *Mission Trends, No. 1*, pp. 59f.

52. Hodgson, *Winds*, pp. 330f.

53. Hoo-Jung Lee, 'Experiencing the Spirit in Wesley and Macarius', in Maddox, *Rethinking Wesley's Theology*, p. 205.

54. Nelson Mandela, *Long Walk to Freedom*, London: Abacus 1996, p. 751.

Select bibliography

General theology

Barth, Karl, *Church Dogmatics*, II.1, Edinburgh: T&T Clark, 1963.

Barth, Karl, *Church Dogmatics*, II.2, Edinburgh: T&T Clark, 1957.

Barth, Karl, *Church Dogmatics*, III.2, Edinburgh: T&T Clark, 1960.

Barth, Karl, *Church Dogmatics*, III.4, Edinburgh: T&T Clark, 1961.

Barth, Karl, *Church Dogmatics*, IV.1, Edinburgh: T&T Clark, 1961.

Barth, Karl, *Church Dogmatics*, IV.4, Edinburgh: T&T Clark, 1969.

Bradley, Ian, *God Is Green*, London: London: Darton, Longman & Todd, 1990.

Bradley, Ian, *The Power of Sacrifice*, London: Darton, Longman & Todd, 1995.

Brunner, Emil, *The Christian Doctrine of God: Dogmatics*, Vol. 1, London: Lutterworth Press, 1964.

Calvin, John, *Institutes of the Christian Religion*, The Library of Christian Classics, Vol. XX, London: SCM Press, 1961.

Davis, Stephen (ed.), *Encountering Evil*, Edinburgh: T&T Clark, 1981.

Dulles, Avery, *Models of the Church: A Critical Assessment of the Church in All Its Aspects*, Dublin: Gill & MacMillan, 1983.

Forsyth, P. T., *The Justification of God*, London: Hodder & Stoughton, 1906.

Fox, Matthew, *Original Blessing*, New Mexico: Bear & Co., 1983.

Langdon Gilkey, *Message and Existence*, London: SCM Press, 1979.

Girard, René, *I See Satan Fall like Lightning*, Leominster: Gracewing, 2001.

Girard, René, *Things Hidden since the Foundation of the World*, London: Athlone Press, 1987.

Grey, Mary, *The Outrageous Pursuit of Hope*, London: Darton, Longman & Todd, 2000.

Mary Grey, *The Wisdom of Fools*, London: SPCK, 1995.

Hodgson, Peter, *Winds of the Spirit*, London: SCM Press, 1994.

Lash, Nicholas, *Theology on the Way to Emmaus*, London: SCM Press, 1986.

MacIntyre, Alasdair, *After Virtue: A Study in Moral Theory*, London: Duckworth, 1981.

Select Bibliography

MacIntyre, Alasdair, *Three Rival Versions of Moral Enquiry: Encyclopaedia, Genealogy, and Tradition*, Indiana: University of Notre Dame Press, 1990.

Moltmann, Jürgen, *The Church in the Power of the Spirit*, London: SCM Press, 1977.

Moltmann, Jürgen, *The Crucified God*, London: SCM Press, 1974.

Moltmann, Jürgen, *The Future of Creation*, London: SCM Press, 1979.

Moltmann, Jürgen, *Theology and Joy*, London: SCM Press, 1973.

Moltmann, Jürgen, *Theology of Hope*, London: London: SCM Press, 1967.

Moltmann, Jürgen, *The Trinity and the Kingdom of God*, London: SCM Press, 1983.

Polkinghorne, John, *Science and Christian Belief: Theological Reflections of a Bottom-UpThinker*, London: SPCK, 1994.

Primavesi, Anne, *From Apocalypse to Genesis*, London: Burns & Oates, 1991.

Robinson, John, *Truth Is Two-Eyed*, London: SCM Press, 1979.

Sacks, Jonathan, *The Dignity of Difference: How to Avoid the Clash of Civilizations*, New York: Continuum Publishing, 2002.

Sacks, Jonathan, *The Dignity of Difference: How to Avoid the Clash of Civilizations*, revd edn, New York: Continuum Publishing, 2003.

Schreiter, Robert, *Constructing Local Theologies*, London: SCM Press, 1985.

Torrance, T. F., *Theological Science*, London: Oxford University Press, 1969.

Volf, Miroslav, *Exclusion and Embrace: A Theological Exploration of Identity, Otherness, and Reconciliation*, Nashville: Abingdon Press, 1996.

Williams, Rowan, *Writing in the Dust: Reflections on the 11th September and Its Aftermath*, London: Hodder & Stoughton, 2002.

Bible and history

Albright, W., and C. S. Mann, *Matthew: Introduction, Translation and Notes*, New York: Doubleday, 1971.

Bruce, F. F., *The Book of the Acts*, London: Marshall Morgan & Scott, 1965.

Bruce, F. F., *The Spreading Flame*, Exeter: Paternoster Press, 1958.

Brueggemann, Walter, *The Covenanted Self*, Minneapolis: Fortress Press, 1999.

Brueggemann, Walter, *Old Testament Theology: Essays on Structure, Theme, and Text*, Minneapolis: Fortress Press, 1992.

Brueggemann, Walter, *Texts That Linger, Words That Explode*, Minneapolis: Fortress Press, 2000.

Cranfield, C. E. B., *The Epistle to the Romans*, Vol. 1, ICC, Edinburgh: T&T Clark, 1975.

Cranfield, C. E. B., *The Gospel according to St. Mark*, The Cambridge Greek Testament Commentary, Cambridge: Cambridge University Press, 1955.

Dunn, James D. G., *Unity and Diversity in the New Testament*, London: SCM Press, 1977.

Goulder, M., *A Tale of Two Missions*, London: SCM Press, 1994.

Hahn, F., *Mission in the New Testament*, London: SCM Press, 1965.

Hamilton, Victor P., *The Book of Genesis, Chapters 1–17*, Grand Rapids: Eerdmans, 1990.

Latourette, K. S., *A History of the Expansion of Christianity*, Vol. II, London: Eyre & Spottiswoode, 1939.

Latourette, K. S., *A History of the Expansion of Christianity*, Vol. IV, London: Eyre & Spottiswoode, 1947.

Neill, Stephen, *A History of Christian Missions*, Harmondsworth: Penguin Books, 1971.

Senior, D., and C. Stuhlmueller, *The Biblical Foundations for Mission*, London: SCM Press, 1983.

Tidball, Derek, *An Introduction to the Sociology of the New Testament*, Exeter: Paternoster Press, 1983.

Mission and theology of mission

Anderson, G., and T. Stransky (eds), *Mission Trends, No. 1*, Toronto: Paulist Press; Grand Rapids: Eerdmans, 1974.

Anderson, G., and T. Stransky (eds), *Mission Trends, No. 2*, Toronto: Paulist Press; Grand Rapids: Eerdmans, 1975.

Anderson, G., and T. Stransky (eds), *Mission Trends, No. 3*, Toronto: Paulist Press; Grand Rapids: Eerdmans, 1979.

Anderson, G., and T. Stransky (eds), *Mission Trends, No. 5*, Toronto: Paulist Press; Grand Rapids: Eerdmans, 1981.

Ariarajah, Wesley, *The Bible and People of Other Faiths*, Risk Book Series, Geneva: WCC, 1985.

Arias, Mortimer, *Announcing the Reign of God: Evangelization and the Subversive Memory of Jesus*, Philadelphia: Fortress Press, 1984.

Bosch, D., *Believing in the Future: Towards a Missiology of Western Culture*, Valley Forge: Trinity Press International, 1995.

Bosch, David, *Transforming Mission: Paradigm Shifts in Theology of Mission*, Maryknoll, NY: Orbis Books, 1998.

Select Bibliography

Bosch, David, *Witness to the World: The Christian Mission in Theological Perspective*, London: Marshall Morgan & Scott, 1980.

Bria, Ion (ed.), *Go Forth in Peace: Orthodox Perspectives on Mission*, WCC Mission Series, Geneva: WCC, 1986.

Butler, Barbara, and Tom Butler, *Just Mission*, London: Mowbray, 1993.

Comblin, José, *The Meaning of Mission*, Dublin: Gill & Macmillan, 1979.

Costas, Orlando, *Christ outside the Gate*, Maryknoll, NY: Orbis Books, 1984.

Cotterell, Peter, *Mission and Meaninglessness*, London: SPCK, 1990.

Cox, Harvey, *Fire from Heaven: The Rise of Pentecostal Spirituality and the Reshaping of Religion in the Twenty-First Century*, London: Cassell, 1996.

Drummond, Richard Henry, *Towards a New Age in Christian Theology*, Maryknoll, NY: Orbis Books, 1985.

Finney, John, *Recovering the Past*, London: Darton, Longman & Todd, 1996.

Fung, Raymond, *The Isaiah Agenda*, Risk Book Series, Geneva: WCC, 1995.

Gallagher, Michael, *Clashing Symbols: An Introduction to Faith and Culture*, London: Darton, Longman & Todd, 1997.

Gibellini, Rosino, *The Liberation Theology Debate*, London: SCM Press, 1987.

Hesselgrave, David, *Communicating Christ Cross-Culturally*, Allahabad: St Paul Publications, 1978.

Hoekstra, Harvey T., *Evangelism in Eclipse*, Exeter: Paternoster Press, 1979.

Jenkins, Philip, *The Next Christendom: The Coming of Global Christianity*, Oxford: Oxford University Press, 2002.

Messer, Donald, *A Conspiracy of Goodness*, Nashville: Abingdon Press, 1992.

Moorhouse, Geoffrey, *The Missionaries*, London: Eyre Methuen, 1973.

Newbigin, Lesslie, *The Open Secret*, Grand Rapids: Eerdmans, 1981.

Padilla, René, *Mission between the Times*, Grand Rapids: Eerdmans, 1985.

Pope Paul VI, *Evangelii Nuntiandi*, Boston: Pauline Books and Media, 2002.

Samuel, Vinay, and Albrecht Hauser (eds), *Proclaiming Christ in Christ's Way: Studies in Integral Evangelism*, Oxford: Regnam Books, 1989.

Scherer, J., and S. Bevens (eds), *New Directions in Mission and Evangelization 1: Basic Statements 1974–1991*, Maryknoll, NY: Orbis Books, 1992.

Stuckey, Tom, *Rainbow, Journey and Feast: Biblical Covenants and a Theology of Mission*, Delhi: ISPCK, 1988.

Sullivan, Emanuel, *Baptised in Hope*, London: SPCK, 1980.

Sundkler, Bengt, *The World of Mission*, London: Lutterworth Press, 1965.

Taylor, John V., *The Go-Between God*, London: SCM Press, 1972.

Thangaraj, M. Thomas, *The Common Task: A Theology of Christian Mission*, Nashville: Abingdon Press, 1999.

Verkyl, J., *Contemporary Missiology*, Grand Rapids: Eerdmans, 1978.

Asian theology

Balasuriya, Tissa, *Eucharist and Human Liberation*, London: SCM Press, 1979.

Balasuriya, Tissa, *Planetary Theology*, London: SCM Press, 1984.

Commission on Theological Concerns of the Christian Conference of Asia (eds), *Minjung Theology: People as Subjects of History*, Maryknoll, NY: Orbis Books, 1981.

Gorringe, Timothy, *Love's Sign: Reflections on the Eucharist*, Madurai: TamilNadu Theological Seminary, 1986.

Griffiths, Bede, *The Cosmic Revelation*, Bangalore: Asian Trading Corporation, 1985.

Griffiths, Bede, *The Marriage of East and West*, London: Fount, 1983.

Griffiths, Bede, *Return to the Centre*, London: Fount Paperbacks, 1978.

Joseph, M., and M. Zachariah (eds), *Discipleship as Mission*, Kottayam: A & A Printers Private Ltd, 1984.

Kitamore, K., *The Theology of the Pain of God*, London: SCM Press, 1966.

Pieris, Aloysius, *An Asian Theology of Liberation*, Edinburgh: T&T Clark, 1988.

Pieris, Aloysius, *Love Meets Wisdom: A Christian Experience of Buddhism*, Maryknoll, NY: Orbis Books, 1988.

Rodrigo, Michael, 'Bible and the Liberation of the Poor', *Dialogue*, XV (1–3) (1988).

Rodrigo, Michael, 'Buddhism and Christianity: Towards the Human Future', *Dialogue*, XIII and XIV (1986–7).

Rodrigo, Michael, 'Liberation: Praxis', *Liberation Theology*, *Logos*, 24 (1) (March 1985), Colombo: Centre for Society and Religion.

Rodrigo, Michael, 'The Moral Passover from Selfishness to Selflessness in Christianity and the Other Religions in Sri Lanka', in *Fr. Mike and His Thought*, *Logos*, 27 (3) (September 1988), Colombo: Centre for Society and Religion.

Rodrigo, Michael, *Tissues of Life and Death*, Colombo: Centre for Society and Religion, 1988.

Rodrigo, Michael, 'Towards a More Intensive Dialogue with Buddhists', *Dialogue*, XII (1–3) (1985).

Sahi, Jyoti, *Stepping Stones*, Bangalore: Asian Trading Corporation, 1986

Song, C. S., *The Compassionate God*, London: SCM Press, 1982.

Song, C. S., *Third-Eye Theology*, Guildford and London: Lutterworth Press, 1980.

African perspectives

Gruchy, John de, *Reconciliation: Restoring Justice*, London: SCM Press, 2002.

Guma, Mogezi, and Leslie Mitton (eds), *An African Challenge to the Church in the 21st Century*, Cape Town: Salty Print, 1997.

Donovan, Vincent J., *Christianity Rediscovered*, London: SCM Press, 1978.

Hulley, Leonard, Louise Kretzschmar and Luke Lungile Pato (eds), *Archbishop Tutu: Prophetic Witness in South Africa*, Cape Town: Human & Rousseau, 1996.

Kingsolver, Barbara, *The Poisonwood Bible*, London: Faber & Faber, 1999.

Krog, Antjie, *Country of My Skull*, London: Jonathan Cape, 1999.

Mandela, Nelson, *Long Walk to Freedom*, London: Abacus, 1996.

Tutu, Desmond, *No Future without Forgiveness*, Johannesburg: Rider Books, 1999.

Britain and the Church in the West

Bailie, Gil, *Violence Unveiled: Humanity at the Crossroads*, New York: Crossroad, 1997.

Bartholomew, C., and T. Moritz (eds), *Christ and Consumerism*, Carlisle: Paternoster Press, 2000.

Bebbington, D.W., *Evangelicalism in Modern Britain*, London: Unwin Hyman, 1988.

Brown, Callum, *The Death of Christian Britain*, London and New York: Routledge, 2001.

Drane, John, *The McDonaldization of the Church*, London: Darton, Longman & Todd, 2001.

Drane, John, *What Is the New Age Saying to the Church?*, London: Marshall Pickering, 1991.

Heslam, Peter, *Globalization: Unravelling the New Capitalism*, Cambridge: Grove Books, 2002.

James, Lawrence, *The Rise and Fall of the British Empire*, London: Abacus, 2000.

Landes, David, *The Wealth and Poverty of the Nations*, London: Little, Brown and Co., 1998.

Leech, Kenneth, *The Sky Is Red: Discerning the Signs of the Times*, London: Darton, Longman & Todd, 1997.

Leech, Kenneth, *Struggle in Babylon: Racism in the Cities and Churches of Britain*, London: Sheldon Press, 1988.

Marsh, Clive, *Christianity in a Post-Atheistic Age*, London: SCM Press, 2002.

McGrath, Alister, *The Future of Christianity*, Oxford: Blackwell Publishers, 2002.

Riddell, Michael, *Threshold of the Future*, London: SPCK, 1997.

Spong, J. S., *Why Christianity Must Change or Die*, New York: HarperSanFrancisco, 1998.

Church growth

Costas, Orlando, *The Church and Its Mission: A Shattering Critique from the Third World*, Wheaton, IL: Tyndale House, 1974.

Gibbs, Eddie, *I believe in Church Growth*, London: Hodder & Stoughton, 1981.

Gill, Robin, *Beyond Decline*, London: SCM Press, 1988.

Gill, Robin, *A Vision for Growth*, London: SPCK, 1994.

Hunter III, George, *The Contagious Congregation: Frontiers in Evangelism and Church Growth*, Nashville: Abingdon Press, 1979.

McGavran, Donald, *The Bridges of God*, London: World Dominion, 1955.

McGavran, Donald, *How Churches Grow*, London: World Dominion, 1959.

McGavran, Donald, *Understanding Church Growth*, Grand Rapids: Eerdmans, 1970.

Pointer, Roy, *How Do Churches Grow?*, Basingstoke: Marshalls Paperbacks, 1984.

Wagner, C. Peter, *Church Growth and the Whole Gospel*, San Francisco: Harper & Row, 1981.

The multi-faith context

Amirtham, S., and S. Wesley Ariarajah (eds), *Ministerial Formation in a Multi-Faith Milieu*, Geneva: WCC, 1986.

Select Bibliography

Cracknell, Kenneth, *Towards a New Relationship*, London: Epworth Press, 1986.

Forward, Martin (ed.), *A Great Commission: Christian Hope and Religious Diversity*, New York: Peter Lang, 2000.

Newbigin, Lesslie, *The Gospel in a Pluralist Society*, London: SPCK, 1989.

Methodism

Davies, R., R. George and G. Rupp (eds), *A History of the Methodist Church in Great Britain*, Vol. 3, London: Epworth Press, 1983.

Davies, R., R. George and G. Rupp (eds), *A History of the Methodist Church in Great Britain*, Vol. 4, London: Epworth Press, 1988.

Hunter III, George, *To Spread the Power: Church Growth in the Wesleyan Spirit*, Nashville: Abingdon Press, 1987.

Langford, Thomas A., *Methodist Theology*, London: Epworth Press, 1998.

Logan, James (ed.), *Theology and Evangelism in the Wesleyan Heritage*, Nashville: Kingswood Books, 1994.

Maddox, Randy (ed.), *Rethinking Wesley's Theology for Contemporary Methodism*, Nashville: Kingswood Books,1998.

Rack, Henry, *Reasonable Enthusiast: John Wesley and the Rise of Methodism*, London: Epworth Press, 1989.

Runyon, Theodore, *The New Creation: John Wesley's Theology Today*, Nashville: Abingdon Press, 1998.

Snyder, Howard A., *The Radical Wesley & Patterns of Church Renewal*, Downers Grove, IL: InterVarsity Press, 1980.

Turner, John Munsey, *John Wesley: The Evangelical Revival and the Rise of Methodism in England*, Peterborough: Epworth Press, 2002.

Wakefield, Gordon, *Methodist Spirituality*, Peterborough: Epworth Press, 1999.

Williams, Colin W., *John Wesley's Theology Today*, London: Epworth Press, 1962.

Spirituality and worship

Collinson, Nigel, *The Land of Unlikeness*, Peterborough: Foundery Press, 1996.

Cullmann, O., and F. J. Leenhardt, *Essays on the Lord's Supper*, London: Lutterworth Press, 1958.

Furlong, Monica, *Merton: A Biography*, London: Darton, Longman & Todd, 1985.

Hart, P., and J. Montaldo (eds), *The Intimate Merton*, A Lion Book, Oxford: Lion, 2000.

Mayne, Michael, *Learning to Dance*, London: Darton, Longman & Todd, 2001.

Merton, Thomas, *New Seeds of Contemplation*, Norfolk, CT: New Directions, 1962.

Merton, Thomas, *No Man Is an Island*, London: Burns & Oates, 1955.

Spink, Kathryn, *A Sense of the Sacred*, London: SPCK, 1988.

Index

Index